CW01623524

The Kingdom Factor

The Kingdom Factor

A personal and practical introduction to the good news of the kingdom of God, and its implications for the church and evangelism today

Roger Mitchell

Marshall Pickering

Marshall Morgan and Scott
Marshall Pickering
3 Beggarwood Lane, Basingstoke, Hants RG23 7LP, UK

Copyright © 1986 by Roger Mitchell
First published in 1986 by Marshall Morgan and Scott Publications Ltd
Part of the Marshall Pickering Holdings Group
A subsidiary of the Zondervan Corporation

All rights reserved. No part of this publication may be reproduced, stored in a retrieval system, or transmitted, in any form or by any means, electronic, mechanical, photocopying, recording or otherwise, without the prior permission in writing, of the publisher

British Library CIP Data

Mitchell, Roger
The Kingdom factor : an introduction to living in the Kingdom of God.
1. Christian life
I. Title
248.4 BV4501.2

ISBN: 0 551 01334 6

Text Set in Plantin by Brian Robinson, North Marston, Bucks.

Printed in Great Britain by
Anchor Brendon Ltd,Tiptree, Colchester, Essex.

Fear not, little flock, for it is your Father's good pleasure to give you the kingdom

Luke 12.32

Contents

Chapter 1

Radical Jesus

(i) Finding the way

The Christianity I grew up with made a big issue of the Bible but not so much of Jesus. That's not to say that I am ungrateful for it, or for the nourishment that it provided for our family life. But it wasn't the whole story. At least, that's how it seems to me on reflection. There was a great deal of the Old Testament, especially the law and the sacrifices. There was plenty of Paul. Personal sin was emphasised a lot. Also the Cross and conversion in a limited sort of way. But the emphasis on the life of Jesus was secondary and we had no real understanding of the prophets, neither their specific judgements on Israel's corporate, social sins nor their perspective on restoration and the New Jerusalem. As a result I could never understand the kingdom of God. I remember asking, many times, 'What is the kingdom of God?' but I never got a satisfactory answer. And even as a child it was obvious to me that nobody knew. So I relegated it to the general area of the mysterious that I gathered was part of the nature of Christianity. Someone said that I should put brackets round everything Jesus said about the kingdom, and later on when I was older or in heaven then I'd understand. I don't think I was ever really content with that. After all, a good deal of the Sunday School hymns and choruses linked the kingdom and children.

So I grew up feeling a lack at a deep level. I don't say that bitterly, but it's a stumbling block that many churches have placed in the way of our generation. Telling a young Christian to put brackets around 'the kingdom of God' is like telling a young footballer to forget about the game and just concentrate on ball control. The whole thing tended towards pointlessness.

Except for the evangelists who came to visit our church regularly – annually I think. I don't think they taught the kingdom of God, but they were undeniably in it. They brought it with them when they came. To me it was like fresh air, like another world breaking in to the humdrum boredom of church life. I loved it, lived for it, always tried to hang on to it. But it mainly went when they did. There was big 'Uncle' George who rounded up all the local yobboes, herded them into a hall and locked the doors on the inside while he told them that God was their Father and loved them. I skulked nervously at the back round-eyed. I was scared of them. But George loved them like a father. I don't think any of them became Christians at our place, but they knew the kingdom of God had come near, and so did I. Then there was absent-minded 'Uncle' Reg, so head over heels in love with men and women for Jesus' sake, that he did endless mad things that utterly delighted me, like when he cut two half circles of hardboard to join together and make a map of the world so he could tell us how much God loved it. First he cut right through the hardboard and into his caravan table. Finally as I remember it, he fixed the two halves firmly together and they were too big to take out of the door. And all oblivious to anything but a good laugh at the problems and God's enormous love for kids. Then there was the drastic time when my mother tried to get her own back on the two Open Air missioners who came. She baked them cotton wool cakes in return for their practical jokes and they gave them to a needy old tramp all unsuspecting. I used to imagine that over and over again. And it wasn't so much the shock of the cotton wool but the fact that they should have given their cakes away to needy old men that got to me. I loved that. That was the kingdom of God somehow.

I started to share about Jesus and God's love for people well before I ever had any personal intimacy with God myself. I wanted so much to be like those evangelists. It wasn't so much what they said. I don't think that they said anything very different from the other preachers and speakers I heard all the other Sundays when they weren't around. But it was the whole life style, the spirit with which they lived and loved. And the only way I knew how to get hold of it was to try and copy them. So a few of us youngsters got to skipping church and buttonholing passers-by in the main street with tracts and discussions about God, as positively as we knew how.

It was during this stage that I first personally encountered the Jesus I was witnessing to. I was seventeen and trying desperately to work out what to do with my life. The church offered little practical guidance. Church life and the world didn't seem to link. On the whole people in the church didn't appear fundamentally different from the rest of the people who never came near it, only more religious. So as a teenager my main hopes for the future were founded on the same faith in money and material advance that the rest of post-war Britain was staking its future on. And I was afraid, fearful of failing to make it in the rat race; of choosing the wrong job, of having no money. So one night in my bedroom, alone, I decided that if God really did love me, this was where he came in. Should I leave school or try and stay on, that was the issue: and whichever got me the best job and the most money. 'Please God, show me what to do . . . ' And the room filled with the sweetness of God's presence and at last my personal experience synchronised with what the evangelists brought.

That same reality of God's love, of jubilation, of a future; the kingdom of God which the evangelists had, came to me. I picked up a Bible and opened it willy-nilly, bingo style. It fell open at Isaiah chapter fifty-five:

> 'Ho, every one who thirsts, come to the waters; and he who has no money, come buy and eat! Come, buy wine and milk without money and without price. Why do you spend your money for that which is not bread, and your labour for that which does not satisfy? Hearken diligently to me, and eat what is good, and delight yourself in fatness.
>
> Incline your ear, and come to me; hear, that your soul may live; and I will make with you an everlasting covenant, my steadfast, sure love for David. Behold, I made him a witness to the peoples, a leader and a commander for the peoples.
>
> Behold, you shall call nations that you know not, and nations that knew you not shall run to you, because of the Lord your God, and of the Holy One of Israel, for he has glorified you.
>
> Seek the Lord while he may be found, call upon him while he is near; let the wicked forsake his way, and the unrighteous man his thoughts; let him return to the Lord, that he may have mercy on him, and to our God, for he will abundantly pardon.'

And I knew I wanted nothing but to exalt in the love that was streaming towards me, to live in it and to bring it in everywhere and to everybody. Everything in me that was sin or ignorance or stood in the way, I wanted shot of. And I knew now what I wanted to do. With a few rare exceptions the only people I had come across who had what I now had were evangelists. So I'd better become one. My brain was slightly more agile than my clumsy hands so I stayed on at school and tried to prepare myself.

The following year I went to work washing up in a Christian hotel in Kent. There, for the first time in my life, I made the extraordinary discovery that there were actually whole churches that had what the evangelists had got! Places where the tangible presence of God, great joy and hope for the future, broke continually into the here and now.

A fellow washer-up asked me to a Bible study. It sounded innocuous enough and as I liked her company I went. I had never come across anything like it. The Bible lived. As it had begun to live in my personal experience, now it lived for a whole group. It spoke right into the situations we were in. A tangible love and commitment was between people and it drew me. I felt I belonged in a way I'd never belonged before. A sense of destiny and responsibility for the future pervaded us all. At first I didn't realise that this was church – then I found out about the Sunday meetings. They were amazing to me in those days. To be caught up for hours at a time in the love of God, in songs and prayers, in the flow of other tongues and the music of guitars and tambourines, was heaven on earth compared with anything I'd ever experienced before. Sometimes we would go out into the streets and sing and dance with joy in the Lord. People would stop and stare of course. And some would chat, want to know more. This was infectious. We broke all previous records for fast washing up that season. We'd hurry all the way to the door of the pub function room where the church met.

Then as I stood outside I'd remember all the things that had been against the love of Jesus in my heart and have to clear them before I went in. The presence of God was so real there. They had the kingdom there.

Later that year I went to Lancaster University to study. I went in great trepidation on two accounts. For a start I was frightened stiff of 'the world', of the 'out there' majority whom I'd encountered on the estate where I grew up, at school, and on the streets where we had talked about Jesus to them. I was afraid of their life style, of getting sucked in. It had always been obvious to me that, despite its selfish destructiveness, the secular world was vastly more interesting and attractive than the church I had grown up in. On top of this, there was the academic study; I was afraid of this too, afraid that Christianity would not stand up to reason, that my faith would evaporate. Most unthinkable of all was that the immediacy of the kingdom might go away, that I might lose the presence of God.

Two things happened however. For a start I met, via the Student Christian Union, Christians who loved Christ but had grown up in the world, whose experience had left them more genuinely Biblical than mine. People in whose lives Jesus' prayer in John 17.15 was being fulfilled. 'I do not pray that you should take them out of the world, but that you should keep them from the evil one.' They understood the fashions and habits and values of the secular world. They struggled with evil of course, and some never made it through. It was hard without any really strong expression of God's alternative kingdom to be caught up into. But they understood and experienced more about the wholeness and fulness of life than I did. Mine had been compartmentalised. I was a religious Christian. They were irreligious Christians but much more like

Jesus. They became my friends, and, thank God, one of them became my wife.

As I studied, first of all philosophy and religion and then contemporary literature and society, it became increasingly obvious to me that the world was in dreadful confusion and that most of what everyone was saying was that it didn't make sense, that in the end all the good things were ruined by the bad things. Which is exactly what Jesus said, except he said he was the sense, and that in him all the good things were going to ruin all the bad things. The more I studied, the more obvious it was that only Christianity made sense. Even when I was struggling with the idiocies of theology like Bultmann's form criticism, with its irrational prejudice against the supernatural intervention of God in history, the very gospel 'myths' which he was 'exploding' were laying new foundations of hope and understanding in my mind.

Those were the days of Vietnam and the first stirrings of general awareness of third world poverty. My senior tutor was a Marxist. If it would help further the cause of the proletariat he would stab me in the back, he said. Jesus, I knew, would have washed my feet, and loved me till my heart broke like the thief's on the cross. Hallelujah! I knew he had done just that. Somehow the world had to get a hold of his kingdom.

It was about this time that another evangelist arrived on the scene. I'd first met Roger Forster at the Christian hotel in Kent. Like the rest before him he carried the kingdom with him. The difference with Roger was that what he said explained it. The Old Testament and Paul had a place in what he said, like the Christianity of my past. But the revolutionary distinction was the central place he gave to Jesus in everything he said, and not just his death. The Cross without the rest of Jesus' life is at worst nonsense and at best only partial good news. Roger related Jesus to everything. Everything Jesus did and said was related to everything that anyone ever does or says. He died and rose to forgive our sin but he also died and rose to bring the love life he lived into all our lives and to all the world. 'This is my lovely son in whom I am well pleased.' I found myself agreeing with what the Father has to say about Jesus more profoundly and completely than ever before.

From that time on I gave myself as totally as I could to doing the job of an evangelist. The experience in Kent had made it clear to me that ordinary Christians can do that; you don't necessarily have to do it as a full time job, it's something the whole church is called to. After I graduated I became a school teacher for a while. Then Sue and I got married, did some post graduate studies and both taught. Everything we did strengthened our conviction that the world needed the kingdom even more than ever, and God wanted to give us it; that what Jesus said in Luke chapter twelve was still utterly true, 'Fear not, little flock, it is your Father's good pleasure to give you the kingdom.' Yet even then I didn't really understand what the gospel was. The more I prepared to talk about Jesus to people the less I felt I understood. I knew that Jesus died for our sins and rose again to make us right with God. I'd always known that. But it just seemed like words to me, as if the spiritual reality wasn't in them. It was there for some preachers. Even now I sense the spiritual power of the words as I write them, but at that time I sensed that a great deal of Christianity had lost something really vital. Seeing that I was trying to do the work of evangelism, and people expected me to get results, I determined to discover exactly what the good news I was sharing was all about. As there were four books at the heart of the Bible I'd been brought up with, which I'd studied in Theology seminars, and which were actually called 'the four gospels', it was obvious where to make a start. I resolved to begin with the gospel of John and simply read it how it was, as a simple human being, and let God speak to me, with as few preconceptions as possible. Wow!

Throughout the whole period I have been describing I had lived with a kind of in-built early warning system against heresy and unsoundness that I had developed since early childhood. Although it had taken a slight battering as I moved away from the influence of my home church, it had survived pretty much intact. In fact, most of the influence I received from other evangelical sources both during and subsequent to my student days, only served to confirm my earlier impressions of Christianity. My views on such diverse subjects as the sovereignty of God, alcohol, politics and women, for example, were standard to most conservative evangelical backgrounds. Even my experience of the baptism in the Holy Spirit among the Christians in Kent was held in a kind of theological tension inside me, because I'd been taught that talk of baptism in the Spirit was unbiblical and generally devilish. But when I began to study John's gospel I wondered where I'd been all this time. How could we ever have missed the plain statements of Scripture? Two things began to happen to me. The first was that Jesus himself set off my early warning alarm at full power. Either he was the worst heretic I had ever come across or a great deal of what goes under the name of evangelical Christianity is unsound and unchristian. The second was that I began at last to understand the good news of the kingdom of God which Jesus brought. Thirteen verses into John's gospel and it was one hundred per cent clear that Jesus came to save everybody. 'The true light that enlightens every man was coming into the world.' But not everybody was willing to receive him. 'He came to his own home, and his own people received him not.' So the question of whether you receive power to become a child of God or not, is dependent on your own human will. It is God's will that it should be that way.

> 'But to all who received him, who believed in his name, he gave power to become children of God; who were born, not of blood nor of the will of the flesh nor of the will of man, but of God.'

So the only sense in which God is sovereign in the matter of who becomes a child of God or not, is in the way that he has decided to give the final sovereignty in the matter to each individual. That is God's will. So I concluded, far from being just for the chosen few, the kingdom of God is a set of restored relationships between God and his people freely available from Jesus for those who want it.

Thirty-four verses into John's gospel and it is established that the Father himself declared baptism in the Spirit to be fundamental to Christianity.

> 'He who sent me to baptise with water said to me, "He on whom you see the spirit descend and remain, this is he who baptises in the Holy Spirit."'

This point impressed me so strongly that I studied John the Baptist's introduction to Jesus in each gospel. I was intrigued to discover that only John's gospel mentions that John the Baptist introduced him as 'the Lamb of God who takes away the sin of the world', but all of them emphasise Jesus as the one who will baptise in the Holy Spirit. In Acts chapter one, it is even in Jesus' own words about the kingdom:

> 'To them he presented himself alive after his passion, by many proofs appearing to them during forty days, and speaking of the kingdom of God. And while staying with them he charged them not to depart from Jerusalem, but to wait for the promise of the Father, which, he said, "You heard from me, for John baptised with water, but before many days you shall be baptised in the Holy Spirit".'

That is to say, the kingdom of God is tangibly received and experienced by baptism in the Holy Spirit.

By John chapter two I was expecting the sparks to fly. But even so, the implications of the events of that chapter still amazed me. The first public appearance of Jesus with his disciples, and the first ever sign of the kingdom of God among men and women, consisted in turning six stone jars of holy water into some 1,440 pints of alcoholic wine to rescue a wedding party, for a bunch of people who had already drunk so much that some of them probably couldn't taste it!

> 'The steward of the feast called the bridegroom and said to him, "Every man serves the good wine first; and when men have drunk freely, then the poor wine; but you have kept the good wine until now." This, the first of his signs, Jesus did at Cana in Galilee, and manifested his glory; and his disciples believed in him.'

Here was a group of people struggling to celebrate the marriage relationship which mirrors the kingdom and Jesus steps in with his disciples to help them to do it. It follows that the kingdom of God establishes a new community which positively blesses the old one wherever it is attempting to affirm kingdom values.

After that Jesus went to the heart of the capital city, where the employees and business partners of the religious and political establishment of his day were carrying out their usual exploitative practices, making money out of other people's sin. There he made a whip of cords and demonstrated for all to see that he had come to be the temple, the heart, of a new society where the sin of mankind would be taken away and new relationships of love and justice would be established.

> 'Making a whip of cords, he drove them all, with the sheep and oxen, out of the temple; and he poured out the coins of the money-changers and overturned their tables. And he told those who sold the pigeons, "Take these things away; you shall not make my father's house a house of trade." His disciples remembered that it was written, "Zeal for your house will consume me." The Jews then said to him, "What sign have you to show us for doing this?" Jesus answered them, "Destroy this temple, and in three days I will raise it up!" The Jews then said, "It has taken forty-six years to build this temple, and will you raise it up in three days?" But he spoke of the temple of his body.'

This must mean that the kingdom of God aggressively challenges the activities of establishment religion and political power where they are destructive of God's values.

Now this is not exactly your 'gentle Jesus meek and mild' kind of Christianity. Or rather it is, but not what those words have come to convey in most circles today. It is what the world needs, I knew that. But what was I going to do with good news about this kind of Jesus in the church? What effect would it have on the established Christian leaders who preside over some of today's churches?

It was time to move on to John chapter three. A respected religious and political establishment figure who had observed Jesus' behaviour in Jerusalem visited him. To be fair, Nicodemus didn't belong to the party responsible for the temple trade. But he obviously hadn't done much to stop it. Perhaps he secretly honoured Jesus for the stand he had been taking. Whatever, Jesus spoke boldly and directly to the root issue. The kingdom of God is not simply a matter of outward words or signs. The heart of the kingdom is neither theology nor political action. It is a spiritual kingdom which we all need to receive.

> 'Truly, truly, I say to you, unless one is born of water and the Spirit, he cannot enter the kingdom of God. That which is born of flesh is flesh, and that which is born of Spirit is spirit.'

And if Nicodemus had accepted the responsibility of being a leader of the people, he ought to have understood it.

> 'Jesus answered him, "Are you a teacher of Israel, and yet you do not understand this? Truly, truly I say to you, we speak of what we know, and bear witness to what we have seen; but you do not receive our testimony."'

Yet the movement of God's outpoured love, forgiving, healing, saving, overcoming evil, has ever been at the beart of what God is doing in the world and certainly does have world changing theological and political effects. So Jesus reminded Nicodemus of Jewish history, of how God asked the Jews to be his channel to eradicate the love-denying practices of the Canaanite people, who honoured relentless materialism, sexual perversion and child sacrifice at the very heart of their national culture and life style. Of how the Jewish people failed to trust God and his supernatural resources and began to be destroyed themselves. How God saved them by the fiery serpent on a pole that stood for the fire of God's Spirit to destroy evil and Satan. And how he gave them a well of water springing up in the desert, speaking of his Spirit welling up to renew them for the job. All this lay behind Jesus' quotation to Nicodemus in John 3.14:

> 'And as Moses lifted up the serpent in the wilderness, so must the Son of Man be lifted up, that whoever believes in him may have eternal life. For God so loved the world that he gave his only Son, that whoever believes in him should not perish but have eternal life'

which life, either then or later, Nicodemus received. So the kingdom comes when the truth is spoken lovingly to the heart of establishment leaders without deference to their intellectual and social standing.

By the time I had got three quarters of the way down chapter four I realised for certain that the good news of Jesus was always going to be more welcome in the world than in many churches I've come across, that is, unless they change. Jesus came to a well. He asked a Samaritan woman for a drink from it. At the same time he offered her the living water of the Spirit. It was all wrong. She was a woman; Jewish men didn't talk to women alone. He was a Jew, she a Samaritan, a racial mixture despised by Jews. He was the son of David, the lion from Judah, she was still worshipping at the defiled shrines of the old northern kingdom of Israel. He was Holy God in the flesh, she was a virtual whore that not even Samaritan women would draw water with. Yet he asked her for a drink and offered her his kingdom! She received it gladly and became the first person to have a direct revelation from Jesus himself as to who he was. As a result, many Samaritans believed. So the Lord of the kingdom loves outcast sinful women of the wrong race and makes Christian leaders and evangelists out of them!

All this and I was only four chapters into John's gospel!

(ii) Understanding the way

The way of the Lord and the kingdom of God are the same thing and both are revealed in Jesus. Let's look at this more closely. Matthew tells us in the third chapter of his good news that John the Baptist preached in the wilderness of Judea, 'Repent, for the kingdom of heaven is at hand.' This, Matthew says, is the fulfilment of Isaiah's prophecy:

> 'The voice of one crying in the wilderness:
> Prepare the way of the Lord, make his paths straight.'

Now, if Matthew is right (which is not in question), 'Repent, for the kingdom of heaven is at hand' is equal to and means the same as 'Prepare the way of the Lord, make his paths straight.' 'Repent' is obviously to 'prepare' and 'make his paths straight'. Therefore 'the way of the Lord' and 'the kingdom of heaven' are the same thing. As the expresssions 'the kingdom of heaven' and 'the kingdom of God' are used interchangeably in the gospels, and as the Lord that John the Baptist prepared the way for is Jesus, we can conclude decisively that the way of Jesus and the kingdom of heaven or God are the same thing.

So, if we want to understand the kingdom of God, all we need to do is to see what Jesus said and did throughout his ministry, and that's it! Now although this makes the gospel rather big, because the good news of the kingdom becomes Jesus himself and everything that he ever said or did, it also makes it quite simple and understandable. In fact it all seems sane and obvious and something that anyone could understand, which it is.

But there is a further important implication, which is that the four gospels become absolutely vital to Christianity. For they describe the Lord's way of doing things, his kingdom. In fact, as John's gospel makes clear, they reveal the very personality and nature of God, for Jesus is the Word, God's self disclosure, the uncovering of who he is and what he wants. As John chapter one puts it, 'No one has ever seen God; the only Son, who is in the bosom of the Father, he has made him known.' Now this most definitely makes the gospels the primary Christian documents within the whole Bible. Which of course explains why Satan's strategy is to attack the historicity and integrity of the gospel records (and why the first task of theology should be to recover and maintain our confidence in their reliability). This is of crucial importance to interpreting and applying the rest of the Bible. It means, without question, that the Old Testament only becomes Christian teaching when it is seen and expounded through the lens of Jesus and the gospels. Similarly, the rest of the New Testament cannot be understood properly unless we follow the process that the New Testament writers followed. They understood the Old Testament scriptures in the light of Jesus as the Holy Spirit brought back to them everything he had said and done, just as promised in John 14.26. Then they applied what they learnt to the situation they were in. With the New Testament as with the Old, the only really accurate process for understanding the Bible is first to understand Jesus and the gospels and then to explain everything else in his light. This is not to say that studying the Old Testament won't help us to understand Jesus, for the Old Testament scriptures prepare the way for him. But at the end of the day it must be what Jesus says and does that determines our understanding of them, and not vice versa. One of the greatest threats to the kingdom today is the same error that the ancient Jews themselves made: that is, to attempt to understand and apply the scriptures in the flesh, and not in the Spirit. That way they virtually lost their destiny in bringing in the kingdom of God in a welter of hypocritically kept outward laws and religious observances. The same influence was at work in the Judaizers of the early days of the church, and it is the same influence that reduces Christianity to boredom and powerlessness in many churches today. The great issue for the church today is to get a real grip on the good news of the kingdom.

There are over eighty separate references to the kingdom of God in the four gospels. This is apart from the places where the gospel writers repeat one another. From these it is easy to discover that Jesus talks about the kingdom in three related but different ways. Firstly, he speaks of the kingdom in relation to his own bodily presence right there in the first century. This is clear on numerous occasions. When in Mark 1.15 Jesus says that the kingdom of God is 'at hand' he does not mean that it is coming soon in time: he means that it is literally close by geographically. The phrase is used repeatedly in this way throughout the gospels. It is the phrase used later by Jesus when he says in Matthew 26.46: 'See, my betrayer is at hand', and in Luke 19.41, when he tells how Jesus came close to the city of Jerusalem and wept over it. The kingdom is close when Jesus is close. You get just the same idea in Matthew 12.28 when Jesus tells his critics, 'If it is by the Spirit of God that I cast out demons, then the kingdom of God has come upon you.' It comes again in Luke 17.21 when Jesus tells the Pharisees,'the kingdom of God is in the midst of you', and in John 3.3–6, when Jesus speaks of the kingdom as something Nicodemus could see and enter in the present, if he would.

Secondly, Jesus refers to the kingdom in its coming universal fulfilment, as with the warning to false followers in Matthew 7.21, or in the parable of the sheep and the goats in Matthew 25.31–34:

> 'When the Son of Man comes in his glory and all the angels with him . . . then the king will say to those at his right hand "Come, O blessed of my Father, inherit the kingdom prepared for you from the foundation of the world".'

Thirdly Jesus refers to the kingdom as present in the lives of his disciples both in the first century and right now and until the final consummation when it will come in universally and forever. As when Jesus gives the challenging promise to his disciples in Matthew 16.28, 'Truly I say to you, there are some standing here who will not taste death before they see the Son of Man coming in his kingdom', or as Mark 9.1 has it, 'before they see the kingdom of God come with power.' This is what the Father's good pleasure is in Luke 12.32: 'to give you the kingdom.'

Put simply, the kingdom of God came into the world with the Lord Jesus, on whom the Spirit 'descended and remained', was shared with those who followed him, was established as undefeatable and permanent by the cross and resurrection, and passed to Jesus' disciples who became his body on earth with the outpouring or baptism in the Holy Spirit at Pentecost. The kingdom continues in the Holy Spirit and through those who continue in the Spirit today. Through their lives it pours ever onwards as the good news is heralded throughout the whole world, and when that work is finished then the end will come. Then the kingdom of the world will become the kingdom of our God and his Christ, and he will reign for ever. There are some references to the kingdom that we can't immediately decide where to fit in, but once this continuum is accepted it's not too difficult to locate them somewhere along the line.

Jesus doesn't only talk about his good news in terms of the kingdom of God. He uses other descriptions for the ways in which the Father is working to bless mankind. Notably he speaks of salvation and eternal life. Mark chapter ten is very helpful in using these different expressions interchangeably within a short space. First of all Jesus is speaking about 'the kingdom of God' in terms of the need to enter it like a child. Then up comes a rich man asking what he must do to inherit 'eternal life.' Afterwards Jesus tells his disciples how hard it is for a rich man to enter 'the kingdom of God.' In astonishment they reply, 'Then who can be "saved"?' But even in these few verses Jesus' preference for speaking in terms of the kingdom of God is obvious. The great advantage of the phrase is its size and scope. 'Eternal life' can be reduced to a vague idea of some sort of after life. It is certainly not how Jesus used it, but it comes down to that in some contexts today. Even 'salvation', which is really a hugely rich word, gets reduced just to the avoidance of hell or a ticket for heaven. But the idea of a kingdom is so big that it gives the lie to a little gospel or a hole-in-the-corner kind of Christianity.

A kingdom must have at least three aspects to it. It must have a king, citizens and possessions or lands. Otherwise it is not a kingdom. There are no kingless kingdoms. There are no one- or even two-man kingdoms. There are no landless kingdoms. So the kingdom of God must have a king, citizens and a place and possessions to reign over. In the good news of the kingdom Jesus announces reconciliation with God the king as our father, peace to mankind as our brothers and sisters, and reconciliation with creation as its heirs, its princes and princesses. Put another way, in the gospel, Jesus offers to establish us as a new creation of people, right with God, right with one another and right with everything else. The only condition is that we repent and believe, receive this good news. This is enormous good news which leaves none of reality untouched. It is simple enough to understand but will take an eternal lifetime to exhaust.

As a human race both individually and corporately we have two great needs. Firstly, we need to be forgiven. Forgiven for what we have done to a heavenly father who loves us to the depths of reality; forgiven for what we have done to ourselves in devaluing such love; forgiven for what we have done to one another by selfishness and dishonour; and forgiven for exploiting, polluting and subjecting God's wonderful creation to death and decay. Secondly, we need life: to be re-created to please our father, to love, serve and honour our fellow men and women, and to have the positive rule and dominion over the earth that God originally intended for us. The good news is full forgiveness from God, man and creation, because in Jesus God was experiencing what sin does to all three; and it is the full weight of God's everlasting love, all that is in the heart of eternity, Father, Son and Holy Spirit, freely shared with you and me.

The good news of the kingdom of God is Jesus' glorious relationship with God the Father as it unfolds through the gospels, offered freely to us, indissoluble since the Cross and resurrection, as in Matthew 11.27, 'No one knows the Father except the Son and any one to whom the Son chooses to reveal him.' And in Luke 11.2, 'When you pray, say: "Father".' And then before the Cross in Mark 14.36,

'Abba Father, all things are possible to you; remove this cup from me; yet not what I will but what you will.' And so the Father's loving lamb-like heart is laid bare in his son and in our world. As Paul puts it in Romans 5.2, 'through him we have access to this grace in which we stand, and we rejoice in our hope of sharing the glory of God.'

But then the good news of the kingdom is also the Father's undying love for all mankind revealed in Jesus' love for Jew and Gentile alike, as with the centurion in Matthew 8.10–13, when he said 'Truly I say to you, not even in Israel have I found such faith . . . be it done for you as you have believed'; seen in his love for poor and rich, like the penniless paralytic at Bethesda who he picked out and healed, and the selfish rich young ruler whom he looked at and loved. And again, in his revolutionary love for women like the Samaritan, the prostitute who washed his feet, and those he included among his disciples and ultimately elevated as the apostles of the resurrection. An indestructible love which, even as he hung in the ultimate rejection of the cross, drew together men and women, Jew and Gentile, rich and poor. As Paul again grasps it in Ephesians 2.18, he made peace through the cross, 'for in him we both have access in one Spirit to the Father'; and in Galatians 3.28, 'There is neither Jew nor Greek, there is neither slave nor free, there is neither male nor female; for you are all one in Christ Jesus.'

And finally, the good news of the kingdom is of restoration for all creation as the sons of God take hold of the kingdom Jesus has secured for them: the kingdom seen as Jesus healed the sick, raised the dead, cast out the demons, calmed the storm; a kingdom seen in power at the cross when the darkness of eclipse was dispelled, the earth quaked, the graves opened and many of the dead were raised along with the Lord Jesus. Paul spells it out in

Colossians 1.19–20:

> 'For in him all the fulness of God was pleased to dwell, and through him to reconcile to himself all things, whether on earth or in heaven, making peace by the blood of his cross.'

And yet again in Romans 8.14–21:

> 'For all who are led by the Spirit of God are sons of God. For you did not receive the spirit of slavery to fall back into fear but you have received the spirit of sonship. When we cry, "Abba! Father!" it is the Spirit himself bearing witness with our spirit that we are children of God . . . for the creation waits with eager longing for the revelation of the sons of God . . . for the creation itself will be set free from its bondage to decay and obtain the glorious liberty of the children of God.'

The creation is not wholly free yet, the kingdom of love isn't yet in all the earth, and we love the Father only feebly. But in Jesus, the Father's love has been perfectly revealed, mankind has been loved to the depths of death, and the beginnings of the new creation have been demonstrated even in the brokenness of our world. And God has invested all of this in the Holy Spirit whom he has freely given to us if we will receive him. We are those on whom the ends of the ages have come: the age of heaven, the New Jerusalem, the kingdom of God where there is no more death, nor mourning, nor crying, nor pain comes to us, touches us, in the now, in the Holy Spirit. Zechariah's glorious prophecy in chapter nine is being fulfilled.

> 'Rejoice greatly, O daughter of Zion! Shout aloud, O daughter of Jerusalem! Lo, your king comes to you; triumphant and victorious is he, humble and riding on an ass. I will cut off the chariot from Ephraim and the war horse from Jerusalem, and the battle bow shall be cut off, and he shall command peace to the nations; his dominion shall be from sea to sea, and from the river to the ends of the earth.'

Today, in our generation, the Father looks for those who will receive his promise of the kingdom in the Holy Spirit and carry the good news in all the earth. Men and women, who, while pressing on into the Father's love will bring him to thousands of others; who, while giving themselves unconditionally to love and support each other, will reach out in love to the strangers and fatherless and enemies; who, while fighting the battle of faith against sickness and decay and death in their own lives, will reach out to destroy Satan's kingdom in the world around them too. We have got to get this good news of the kingdom into all the earth. God has absolutely set his heart on it.

Chapter 2

Radical Church

(i) The reality of fellowship in the Spirit

The Ichthus Christian Fellowship, of which I am a part, started with about sixteen of us in 1974. It has since grown into an area resource church of around one thousand two hundred people meeting in some fifteen local congregations and over fifty housegroups. It is not something I find easy to write about as it is not mine but belongs corporately to all my brothers and sisters and the Lord. Just as the Lord deals with us as individuals and the personal revelations he gives are the inner strength of our more public lives for him, so it is with the common life the Spirit brings to us. We need to take care not to leak it out all over the place. So I'm not going to say anything in detail of the inside story of our lives together over the years. Perhaps the time will come when the early years will be slipping into history and then some of the joys and pains of our birth and childhood can be written about. Better still, the kingdom of God will be in by then. Nonetheless I will offer no apology for drawing heavily on Ichthus' experience where I feel free to do so. Just as my church days while a youngster have been formative for me, the last ten years within Ichthus have been even more so.

Perhaps I should say something at this point for the

benefit of those whose church experience is like my own used to be, or even who shared those days with me. Maybe they didn't seem so bad at the time and could have been a lot worse; the Lord was not entirely absent and some people did come to him through the filter of what we had together. But my experience of church life these last ten years has so revolutionised my understanding and expectations of fellowship in the Holy Spirit, of Christian leadership, of the growth and mobilisation of the members of the body and the actual possibility of success in the work of the kingdom, that I want to share it even if it hurts. Ichthus has a long way to go; it is not yet the heaven on earth which should be the goal of all churches. And most of London, England and the world still needs evangelising, quite apart from the task we have in front of us in Ichthus of planting another fifty congregations this decade. Nevertheless, what we have got is the evidence that much more can be got hold of in the Holy Spirit than some of us used to think. And even if the unthinkable happens and we lose the future in Ichthus (which we are not contemplating!), what we have had in the Holy Spirit is built everlastingly into the eternal kingdom. This is the positive way of looking at some of our more negative experiences of church life.

I have often thought of the widow whom Jesus commends in Luke 21.1–4 for putting her two copper coins in the temple treasury. It was all coming down under the judgement of God, but what she had put in earned the commendation of Jesus and has therefore been built into the indestructible kingdom of God. We can encourage but not excuse ourselves with that.

I can't remember the exact time that I first started pinching myself in Ichthus worship services to see if I was awake or dreaming! It was the tangible presence of the Lord which, despite those Kent experiences I've mentioned earlier, I found difficult to believe that I was experiencing. I think it was from the earliest days, although the intensity of his presence and the style of our response have developed over the years. This sense of real fellowship, actual partnership, in the Holy Spirit has been increasingly our experience in every area of our corporate life. Those who preach find it rare not really to break through: this is as true in our open air meetings as among the believers. New ventures meet with success – even radical new ideas like our Jesus Action programme for community care. Counselling situations uncover root problems and people move onwards in the Lord. New congregations are planted and grow, and as at the present count, people are becoming Christians virtually every day.

Now the initiative for all this is with God and we praise him for it. But we are not so pretentious about ourselves or dishonouring to God to think that he doesn't want to be present among and bless people like this everywhere. So the question of why there is this much blessing becomes a vital one. The more so because we want to open up our hearts for much greater blessings than even these. I am in no doubt that the answer is with the unity in the Holy Spirit that God has given at the heart of our life together since the beginning. It has not always been painless but it has been wonderful. The writer of Psalm 133 puts it like this:

> 'Behold, how good and pleasant it is when brothers dwell in unity! It is like the precious oil upon the head, running down upon the beard, upon the beard of Aaron, running down on the collar of his robes! It is like the dew of Hermon, which falls on the mountains of Zion! For there the Lord has commanded the blessing, life for evermore.'

The Lord has brought the church, the family of God, into being for two essential purposes. These are like two sides of a coin. On the one hand the church exists for nurture: it is a bulwark, a haven, a city, a fold, for protection from the demonic forces that are out to devalue and destroy the lives of men and women. On the other hand, it is for mission: it is an army, a channel, a light, a highway for God to move down and through for the salvation of the world and the defeat of his enemies. To fulfil either function, of nurture or of mission, the church must be intact. Its foundations and its walls must be strong. The Psalmist compares 'brothers dwelling in unity' with 'the mountains of Zion.' There must be a relationship of united brotherhood at the core of the people of God, among the leadership, if the blessing of life for evermore is to be experienced and maintained.

Two further things need to be said about this. Firstly, all Biblical leadership is corporate, plural. The Godhead is corporate. Throughout history God has called individuals as leaders, but his calling has always led them into or towards a relationship of shared leadership. Even Jesus immediately drew a team of disciples around him as he commenced his ministry. This is because of the nature of what God wants with his kingdom. Individuals in love with him, in common corporate life, sharing the glory of the Godhead, is what God is after. Of course, someone needs to be the first among equals if leadership is to function adequately. One or another will need to be a Peter or Paul or James among the Johns, Marys, Timothys and so on. Just who it should be will be obvious as the Spirit leads through our open hearts. But it must be expressed in ongoing humble love and mutual accountability.

Secondly, this dwelling in unity is not a structural thing, it is spiritual. It is like the precious anointing oil and the dew of Hermon. It is the anointing of the same Holy Spirit whose unity the Father and Son dwell in. This dwelling in unity is variously translated as 'staying', 'abiding' or 'remaining' in the Spirit by the various New Testament translators. This is the unity which the Father told John the Baptist about in John 1.33: 'He on whom you see the Spirit descend and remain, the same is he who baptises in the Holy Spirit', which unity John's erstwhile disciples clamoured to see and experience in John 1.38. So must we.

> 'Jesus turned, and saw them following, and said to them, "What do you seek?" And they said to him, "Rabbi" (which means Teacher), "where are you staying?" He said to them "Come and see." They came and saw where he was staying; and they stayed with him that day, for it was about the tenth hour.'

Jesus dwelt in the Holy Spirit, this was how he was recognised as the baptiser in the Spirit. Now the disciples wanted to share in that same spiritual unity. Jesus is still praying for this at the end of his ministry in John 17.20–21 and praying for us in exactly the same terms:

> 'I do not pray for these only, but also for those who believe in me through their word, that they may all be one; even as you, Father, are in me, and I in you, that they also may be in us, so that the world may believe that you have sent me.'

To live corporately in the spirit like this is the clue to spiritual success, for it is the Father's pleasure and promise that the same anointing Jesus had should be on his followers, his body. Just as he claimed in the synagogue in Luke 4.18–19:

> 'The Spirit of the Lord is upon me, because he has anointed me to preach good news to the poor. He has sent me to proclaim release to the captives and recovering of sight to the blind, to set at liberty those who are oppressed, to proclaim the acceptable year of the Lord.'

This is the inheritance of those whose hearts are open to God and each other. All leaders among God's people must set this goal before them: To know and experience this kind of love and unity in the Holy Spirit at all cost. No one who isn't ready for this should be a leader among the people of God, for this is the common life style for all God's people and God intends their leaders to spread it infectiously around them! If not, the enemy gets in among us. This is why Satan attacks leaders in particular, and why when he succeeds, the damage is so deep and so destructive to people's spirits. James warns us about this in James 3.15-18, identifying jealousy and selfish ambition as the chief underlying causes of any breakdown in fellowship and subsequent loss of the Spirit in corporate life. Commenting on wrong attitudes of heart and evil speaking among leaders, he says:

> 'This wisdom is not such as comes down from above, but is earthly, unspiritual, devilish. For where jealousy and selfish ambition exist, there will be disorder and every vile practice. But the wisdom from above is first pure, then peaceable, gentle, open to reason, full of mercy and good fruits, without uncertainty or insincerity. And the harvest of righteousness is sown in peace by those who make peace.'

God wants us to be established and protected in this true unity in the Spirit 'which comes from above' with the greatest possible care. If we can do it Paul answers us in Ephesians 4.1–8, the church will receive the necessary gifts to play its part in the work of the kingdom.

> 'I . . . beg you to lead a life worthy of the calling to which you have been called, with all lowliness and meekness, with patience, forbearing one another in love, eager to maintain the unity of the spirit in the bond of peace . . . Grace was given to each of us according to the measure of Christ's gift. Therefore it is said, "When he ascended on high he led a host of captives, and he gave gifts to men".'

Actually, doing this is not as difficult as it sounds. For us to have unity in the Spirit we simply need to be continually and unitedly filled with the Spirit. Or put it another way, we need to spend time worshipping God freely together. The basis of both pastoral care and the mission of the church is worship in the Holy Spirit. Our resources for living, forgiveness for sin, and renewal for our minds and bodies are all available in the Holy Spirit. Protection from Satan and attack is all in the Holy Spirit, for God is enthroned on the praises of his people. Power for moving out into the world in witness and warfare is in the Holy Spirit, for God reigns out of the praises of his people. At one time I was prepared to concede that so called charismatic worship was simply one expression of worship among many others. I no longer think that. Worship must be as diversely creative as we can make it. But it must all be charismatic in the sense of opening us up as totally as possible to receive from God in the Holy Spirit with all our being: spirit, soul and body. This kind of worshipping was fundamental to early church life and must still be today if we want to know the overflowing blessings of the Father pouring in and through our lives. When Paul says that we are not to neglect meeting together as some do, it is on a par with his encouragement to married couples not to neglect lovemaking. In fact, the root word for worship in the New Testament is to kiss. He certainly doesn't mean you must do your duty and go along even though it's boring! This link between worship and life in the Spirit is rooted in the teaching of Jesus in John 4.23–24:

> 'The hour is coming, and now is, when the true worshippers will worship the Father in spirit and truth, for such the Father seeks to worship him. God is spirit, and those who worship him must worship in spirit and truth.'

And it is taken up many times by Paul, most clearly in Ephesians 5.18–20:

> 'Be filled with the Spirit, addressing one another in Psalms and hymns and spiritual songs, singing and making melody to the Lord with all your heart, always and for everything giving thanks in the name of our Lord Jesus Christ to God the Father.'

Spending time worshipping the Lord like this, meeting him in one another, remembering his exhortation in Matthew 5.23–24 to be right with our brother before we worship, is the best possible way of glueing a company of Christians together in the Holy Ghost.

(ii) The purpose of fellowship in the Spirit

The purpose of fellowship in the Holy Spirit is that the kingdom of God might come ever more greatly in and through our lives. In order to look at the way this comes about in more detail, it is helpful to notice the terms in which Jesus himself described the fellowship which he wanted to have with his disciples in Mark 3.14–15:

> 'And he went up into the hills, and called to him those whom he desired; and they came to him. And he appointed twelve, to be with him, and to be sent out to preach and have authority to cast out demons.'

Three aspects of the life of the kingdom are clearly focussed on by Jesus here. There is the aspect of fellowship with Jesus for its own sake, 'to be with him.' Then there is the job of bringing the good news of the kingdom to the world, 'to be sent out to preach.' Finally, there is the task of overthrowing Satan's dominion, 'to cast out demons.' Now admittedly this needs unpacking, but here in a nutshell is the whole task of the church. It's important to notice how the three aspects belong together. Jesus desired each of the twelve to do all of these things. These ministries are together the whole task of the church. Some Christians have tended to emphasise one or the other task. But even the ministry of being with Jesus is not at the expense of the rest of the mission of the church. People who have been with Jesus will share his heart for the world and want his victory over his enemies. So nothing I have said about giving time to worship in the Holy Spirit is at the expense of evangelism – far from it. It is on the job of evangelism that we worship. Folk who withdraw from evangelism into worship, who are 'not into evangelism', are misunderstanding the work of the kingdom. But similarly, those who reach out to the world without a base of worship in the Spirit or spiritual warfare, have little or nothing to offer. They might not even be seeing the kingdom of God at all.

Just as Jesus shared these responsibilities with each of the twelve disciples, he intended them to share them in turn with the rest of the church. It is terribly important to grasp this fact if we are to get the good news of the kingdom into all the earth. Jesus didn't share the work of the kingdom just with a few leaders: he chose a manageable few to equip them for the task so that they could share with others, so that ultimately the world's multitudes could share in the kingdom. This is what Jesus was getting at when he encountered the crowds in Matthew 9.35–38:

> 'When he saw the crowds, he had compassion for them, because they were harassed and helpless, like sheep without a shepherd. Then he said to his disciples, "The harvest is plentiful, but the labourers are few; pray therefore the Lord of the harvest to send out labourers into his harvest".'

The aim of the disciples is not simply to serve people or even to bring them to Jesus, but to make them themselves labourers in the harvest; those who will be with Jesus, be sent out to preach and to cast out demons. It is in this context that we need to understand Paul's account of the church's leadership gifts in Ephesians 4.11–12:

> 'And his gifts were that some should be apostles, some prophets, some evangelists, some pastors and teachers, for the equipment of the saints, for the work of the ministry, for building up the body of Christ.'

Now that is how the RSV puts it. But the comma after 'saints' is unwarranted. There is no punctuation in the original Greek. If you take the comma away, you have a vitally important change in meaning which confirms Jesus' emphasis. That is to say, the leadership gifts are given in order that the individuals who have such gifts might themselves be given to the church to equip the whole body for the work of the ministry. They are mobilising gifts 'for the equipment of the saints for the work of the ministry.'

Now if we understand the leadership rôles within the church in this way then the church becomes not a hierarchical or exclusive pyramid but an open-ended arrowhead of mission into the world. Pastors and teachers train people alongside them to pastor and teach, evangelists train evangelists as they go about the work of evangelising, prophets breed prophets as they prophesy and apostles train apostles for the ongoing work of church planting. And this is not the end of it, for the ministries themselves are fluid and progress with the developing work. Pastors and teachers learn to shepherd the sheep who are found, and in so doing prepare themselves for the even more difficult job of shepherding the lost sheep, and become evangelists. Evangelists get so used to relating what God is saying through the gospel to a lost world that they begin to be able to hear and declare what God is saying in specific terms both to the church and the world. And the prophets who now combine the gifts of pastoring and teaching with the ability to win the lost and give overall direction to the church, are able to move out into church planting in an apostolic rôle. So the church is constantly building outwards into the world and giving more and more room for developing leadership and mobilising the saints in the work of the kingdom.

This process is the only thing that makes real sense of the apparent confusion of ministries in the Acts of the Apostles, a wrong understanding of which has often led to restrictive and stereotyped models of church government. Barnabas who is allowed room to exercise his basic gifts of encouragement and generosity in Acts 4.34–37 soon develops pastoral gift as seen in his care of Paul as a new convert in Acts 9.26–27. Later he is sent as a pastor and teacher to Antioch and develops into a gifted evangelist alongside the others there in Acts 11.19–26. Later still he is described as being among the prophets in Antioch and is set aside to do the work of an apostle alongside Paul in Acts 13.1–3. A very similar kind of process can be followed with James the brother of Jesus, Stephen, Philip, Timothy, Priscilla and Aquila and so on. This is how the early church grew, and so it must be today.

It will be clear from all this that 'function', that is, 'doing the job', came before 'structure', that is, 'being called by the name of the job you do.' Even the disciples were following Jesus in the work of fishing men before he selected twelve of them in particular and called them apostles. It is a fundamental mistake when the people of God try to operate the other way round. When this happens the work of the kingdom is constantly held up by the ineptitude or unwillingness of leaders to lead properly. This way the work can be set back for a whole generation because leaders are much easier to appoint than to remove. This simply must not be allowed to go on any longer.

As well as being progressive and flexible in its ministries and structures, the church needs to be progressing in the quality of its kingdom life. As Paul makes clear in 1 Corinthians 10.11, we are those 'upon whom the end of the ages has come' or, more accurately to the original, 'the *ends* of the ages.' In other words, we live in the overlap of the kingdom of this world and the kingdom of God. In that overlap it is our business as the people of God to seek to get as much of the kingdom of heaven into this world as possible until death is swallowed right up in victory and Jesus returns for ever. Then the New Age will be upon us completely. It is with this in view that Jesus taught us to pray in Matthew 6.10, 'Your kingdom come, your will be done, on earth as it is in heaven.' As someone has put it, the work of the kingdom is not so much to get people out of earth into heaven, but to get as much of heaven as possible on to the earth and into people.

In Galatians 3.28 Paul neatly sums up the quality of life in the kingdom of God in terms of the equality of our status in the Lord Jesus. As he puts it, 'There is neither Jew nor Greek, there is neither slave nor free, there is neither male nor female; for you are all one in Christ Jesus.' The first twelve apostles were all Jews, all free and all men. But Jesus' radical teaching and actions prepared the way for the progress of the kingdom in terms of Gentiles, slaves and women as well. At the very beginning of his ministry when he spoke of his anointing in the Spirit in the synagogue of Nazareth, Jesus infuriated the Jews by reminding them of God's care for Sidonians and Syrians. He continued in exactly the same way when he encountered the faith of the Roman centurion in Matthew 8.8–13 and declared:

> 'Truly, I say to you, not even in Israel have I found such faith. I tell you, many will come from east and west and sit at table with Abraham, Isaac and Jacob in the kingdom of heaven, while the sons of the kingdom will be thrown into the outer darkness.'

In many other ways Jesus made his intentions clear until finally he commissioned the eleven in Matthew 28.19, 'Go therefore and make disciples of all nations.'

And so Paul rightly concluded that racial background was no bar to equality in the kingdom of God. Even so it was with a struggle that even the apostles came to accept the idea, for all Jesus' clarity on the subject. Peter shouldn't really have needed special revelation from heaven about it, nor should it have been necessary to call together the Council of Jerusalem in Acts 15, let alone for Paul to have to withstand Peter on the matter. For all that, there have yet been struggles and shameful anti-kingdom actions in the history of the church over racial issues and still are today. This is a grief to the Holy Spirit whenever it happens. So the work of the kingdom must not only progress in quantity in the world but in quality too. Particularly in cosmopolitan and cross-cultural situations such as are found in the major cities of the world, we must work to establish churches that are real expressions of kingdom life, with genuine racial equality in the Holy Spirit.

The Roman centurion whom Jesus commended was a slave owner. In fact, as is clear in Luke's account of the incident in Luke 7.1–10, Jesus' kingdom at that point was not only reaching out to include Gentiles but the Gentiles' slaves. Later Jesus made it clear in Matthew 20.25–28 that those apostles who wanted to be the greatest in the kingdom must learn to become slaves.

> 'Jesus called them to him and said, "You know that the rulers of the Gentiles lord it over them, and their great men exercise authority over them. It shall not be so among you; but whoever would be great among you must be your servant, and whoever would be first among you must be your slave; even as the Son of Man came not to be served but to serve, and to give his life as a ransom for many."'

Not surprisingly again, Paul concluded that economic status was no bar to equality in the kingdom of God, and although his teaching stops short of the radical step of insisting on the abolition of slavery within the church immediately, perhaps because it would have exposed slaves and Christians generally to unnecessary hardship or death in the then current political scene, he wrote to Philemon the slave owner about his runaway slave in such terms that ensured the eventual destruction of slavery within the church.

> 'Perhaps this is why he was parted from you for a while, that you might have him back for ever, no longer as a slave but more than a slave, as a beloved brother, especially to me but now much more to you, both in the flesh and in the Lord. So if you consider me your partner, receive him as you would receive me.'

Once again, since Paul wrote so radically, the church has often been slow to see or accept the need for the kingdom to increase in quality, more faithfully to express heaven and God's way. Not until men like Charles Finney and John Wesley insisted that full Christian commitment necessitated full commitment to the abolition of slavery did the church as a whole begin to progress in the quality of its kingdom life in this respect, despite the fact that the Roman empire had long since given way to a variety of so-called Christian empires and states. We don't have slavery within the church today, but we need to work for the progress of the kingdom among the people of God and out into the world, so that it genuinely becomes the place in which social and economic status is no barrier to equality either for service or for leadership in the Holy Spirit.

Most relevant of all for the church today is the need for the kingdom to progress in giving full equality in the Holy Spirit to women. The good news has so salted society today that there is not the slightest vestige of an argument against the kingdom being demonstrated in the full inclusion of women in leadership of the people of God and in the work of the kingdom. And yet some churches today, even churches openly seeking to move in the Holy Spirit, are so obstructive to the freedom of women that the secular world, far from understanding that the freedom now given to more and more women in wider society is part of the effect of the good news of the kingdom, actually views the church as the last stronghold of male domination. As a result some women are even driven into the strident and often demonic expressions of liberation that counterfeit the kingdom of God. This is a scandal and a slur on the name of Jesus who died to bring women their true inheritance in his kingdom.

Of course none of the first twelve apostles were women. But as we've already seen, none of them were Gentiles or slaves either. Jesus included women in his inner circle of disciples from early days as Luke 8.1–3 shows:

> 'Soon afterward he went on through cities and villages, preaching and bringing the good news of the kingdom of God. And the twelve were with him, and also some women who had been healed of evil spirits and infirmities: Mary, called Magdalene, from whom seven demons had gone out, and Joanna, the wife of Chuza, Herod's steward, and Susanna, and many others, who provided for them out of their means.'

This whole entourage provided an extraordinarily radical statement of the kingdom, when you consider that a Jewish man wasn't even expected to be seen along with a woman, and that women had no part to play in the synagogue. But it wasn't radical enough for Jesus, who arranged things so that the first apostles of the resurrection were women. And the men didn't believe them, as Luke 24.1-12 tells us!

> 'But on the first day of the week, at early dawn, they went to the tomb, taking the spices which they had prepared. And they found the stone rolled away from the tomb, but when they went in they did not find the body. While they were perplexed about this, behold, two men stood by them in dazzling apparel; and as they were frightened and bowed their faces to the ground, the men said to them, "Why do you seek the living among the dead? Remember how he told you, while he was still in Galilee, that the Son of Man must be delivered into the hands of sinful men, and be crucified, and on the third day rise?" And they remembered his words, and returning from the tomb they told all this to the eleven and to all the rest. Now it was Mary Magdalene and Joanna and Mary the mother of James and the other women with them who told this to the apostles; but these words seemed to them an idle tale, and they did not believe them.'

Not too much scope for male pride after that you might have thought! And so from the very first days of the early church this group of women were singled out alongside the eleven and Jesus' brothers, with Mary the mother of Jesus even named alongside the list of the apostles in Acts 1.13-14. Throughout the Acts women had a developing ministry in the life of the church. Lydia had a church in her house in Acts 16.15 and so obviously developed a pastoral ministry. Priscilla, with her husband Aquila was a teacher in Acts 18.26 and later an evangelist and probably eventually an apostle. Paul describes her as his fellow worker in Romans 16.3. Philip in Acts 21.9 had four unmarried daughters who were 'prophesying' in the continuous tense and so presumably were prophetesses with good Old Testament precedent in Deborah and Huldah. By any standards I know, the tone of Romans 16.3–7 implies that Priscilla, Mary and Junia were all apostles and there is certainly no reason why they should not have been. And yet once again in the history of God's people it has been a real struggle for the church, and particlarly male leaders, to accept the rôle of women in the kingdom of God. Passages from Paul's epistles that were clearly written to safeguard women in leadership from hassle, misunderstanding and disgrace, that at the time of writing honoured women in the church, have been used to dishonour and silence them. This too is a grief to the Holy Spirit. Quite obviously verses like 1 Corinthians 14.34 need looking at in context.

> 'The women should keep silence in the churches for they are not permitted to speak, but should be subordinate, as even the law says. If there is anything they desire to know, let them ask their husbands at home. For it is shameful for a women to speak in church.'

Now we can say quite categorically that unless Paul was having a brainstorm only three chapters earlier then a woman can play a leading vocal part in public meetings of the church. Otherwise Paul's whole discussion in 1 Corinthians 11.4–10 of how to protect woman's honour when she is praying or prophesying in public is nonsense. Literally the phrase 'be subordinate' in 1 Corinthians 14.34 means 'under the order.' Women are to be 'under the order' in the same way that prophets are to be 'under the order' in 14.32. Prophets show that they are 'under the order' by 'keeping silent' when another prophet speaks as in 14.28. Therefore the way that women keep silence is to keep silent while others are speaking. This is the whole point. Paul's reference to women in 1 Timothy 2.11–12 is similar and the argument about silence is the same. But he also says 'I permit no woman to teach or to have authority over men.' The word translated 'to have authority' here is unique in the New Testament and is such a very strong word it can actually mean to murder. The AV translation is better: 'to usurp authority.' Paul's point here is that a woman should not use her freedom in the church to teach in such a self assertive way that she devalues and puts down men, which in her new found freedom she might be tempted to do. This clearly is exactly what Priscilla did *not* do to Apollos in Acts 18.24–28 even though in teaching him she was teaching a man who was already eloquent and well versed in the scriptures.

The harder we pray and work for the kingdom to increase in quality the more it will increase in quantity as well. For as all who receive the kingdom are mobilised in the Spirit for the work of the kingdom, including all races, classes and both sexes, so the kingdom will enlarge its hold on the earth.

To sum up, the purpose of fellowship in the Holy Spirit is to produce a loving community, continuously expanding both in the quantity of its members and the quality of its kingdom life, who are close to Jesus and working to bring the good news to all the world by the preaching of the kingdom and by spiritual warfare.

It is to the nature of this preaching of the kingdom and spiritual warfare that the rest of this book is devoted.

Chapter 3

Kingdom Warfare

(i) Discovery and overview

Spiritual warfare is the hidden face of evangelism. This is actually obvious from the life of Jesus, in particular from the context of the temptations, his explanation of the need to bind the strong man in order to see the kingdom come powerfully and his comments to the disciples about why he was successful in casting out a demon when they were not. We shall have a detailed look at all this later. Of course Paul has much to say on this subject too.

But to me the discovery that evangelism is battle was a complete eye opener. When I first went to work in Kent in 1966, immediately prior to my encounter with the living Christians I mentioned in chapter one, I met someone who was so clearly demon possessed and encountered a house that was so full of occult activity that I had to totally revolutionise my thinking. I don't propose to go into details because they are not healthy and in any case involve people and incidents that even after all this time I don't feel free to disclose. Suffice it to say I saw and heard for myself evidence of the demonic that would eclipse any late-night horror film, and so I had to begin to work out how to act as a messenger of the kingdom in that context. I learnt how to hide in the protection of Jesus' blood and in the presence of his Spirit with me. I learnt the power of Jesus' name to bind the forces of darkness even at a distance. No more than that, but it was a beginning. Later I encountered the spiritual battle more positively, as I got involved in student evangelism and university missions. Often universities are built in places which were, and sometimes still are, centres of occult learning and practice. When we proclaimed the good news of the kingdom, particularly when we did so in public places and in the open air, it tended to stir up the demonic forces. Foul occult statements and signs would be written over the mission publicity or pinned on doors and noticeboards. Sometimes we would receive weird and threatening letters and encounter some very frightening people. But parallel to our evangelism which we worked at quite straightforwardly in personal conversations, pizza parties, meetings, concerts, street theatre and so on, we would give ourselves to times of prayer and seek to grow in fellowship in the Holy Spirit, listing the people we had met who showed any real signs of openness to Jesus and praying consistently for them, that they would be released from all that held them back and receive the Lord. Again and again we would see them converted and at times involving quite dramatic deliverances from demonic forces. These days, as we have learnt much more about the nature of the spiritual battle, right here in South East London, these kinds of deliverances are a much more common experience.

From 1980–82 Sue and I served as staff workers with the International Fellowship of Evangelical Students in the South Pacific. We learnt a great deal at that time for which we are indebted to God and to our many brothers and sisters there. Towards the end of our stay we encountered a major onslaught of Satanic attack on the work. Although I had never operated like it before, the Lord showed me clearly that a literal evil spirit was responsible for the confusion that had grown up almost over night among some of the student leaders. As we came against it in the name of the Lord, not only were we able to see the work guarded and delivered from disruption at that time, but some of the ways in which the enemy had penetrated our ranks became obvious from the manifestations that took place when we prayed together.

Now of course this whole area of spiritual warfare is very heavy, which is hardly surprising when you consider just how much evil there is in the world and in the human heart. How did it get there? Satan's power must be strong and deceitful indeed if it can so withstand the purposes of the Father's loving heart and so obstruct his glorious plans for his people and their world. We can't shy away from this one if we are going to share the Father's heart and be the means whereby his enemies are defeated, his kingdom comes, and his will gets done. For this is the rôle of the people of God.

Paul says in Ephesians 3.8–9:

> 'To me, though I am the very least of all the saints, this grace was given, to preach to the Gentiles the unsearchable riches of Christ, and to make all men see what is the plan of the mystery hidden for ages in God who created all things; that through the church the manifold wisdom of God might now be made known to the principalities and powers in the heavenly places.'

John in Revelation 12.10–11 tells of the voice which he heard proclaiming the ultimate defeat of Satan:

> 'Now the salvation and the power and the kingdom of our God and the authority of his Christ have come, for the accuser of our brethren has been thrown

> down, who accuses them day and night before our God. And they have conquered him by the blood of the Lamb and by the word of their testimony, for they loved not their lives even unto death.'

Although it is by the blood of the Lamb and the good news about Jesus that Satan is conquered, these verses make clear that we, the saints, have a crucial part to play in applying Jesus' victory to the enemy and so finally overcoming him.

Following the way of understanding the Bible which I've already outlined in the second part of chapter one, the core incidents for our understanding of spiritual warfare will be those contained in the gospels. We will examine other scriptures in the light of these and in that way build up the picture.

Even a cursory reading of the gospels makes clear that Jesus took for granted the existence of a real personal devil and hosts of demons. He viewed them as of central significance and saw a major part of the work of the kingdom in terms of the release of thousands of men and women whom they held in bondage. This was no theoretical matter. The demons recognised him as really as he recognised them, as in Matthew 8.28–29:

> 'The demoniacs met him, coming out of the tombs, so fierce that no one could pass that way. And behold, they cried out, "What have you to do with us, O Son of God? Have you come here to torment us before the time?"'

Matthew's gospel has over fourteen separate references to the demonic powers of which the following from Matthew 4.24 and 8.16 are typical.

'So his fame spread throughout all Syria, and they brought him all the sick, those afflicted with various diseases and pains, demoniacs, epileptics, and paralytics, and he healed them.'
'That evening they brought to him many who were possessed with demons; and he cast out the spirits with a word.'

Now we need to ask where these demons came from. The Pharisees in Matthew 12.24 were of the opinion that they were in the tow of Beezebul, the prince of demons. Jesus agrees with this, although not with their suggestions that this was where he got his own power over them from. Jesus goes on to make it clear in Matthew 12.25–28 that Beezebul is Satan, or the devil, and that it is by the Spirit of God that he is casting him out.

'Knowing their thoughts, he said to them, "Every kingdom divided against itself is laid waste, and no city or house divided against itself will stand; and if Satan casts out Satan, he is divided against himself; how then will his kingdom stand? . . . But if it is by the Spirit of God that I cast out demons, then the kingdom of God has come upon you."'

Two important points can be made from this. Firstly, to cast out demons and to cast out Satan is the same thing because he is their prince and they represent him. 'If Satan cast out Satan, he is divided against himself.' Secondly, casting out demons is proof of the presence of the kingdom, the breakthrough of heaven into earth, God's will being done, because Satan is not only the prince of demons but also the prince of this world. Now this is something that Jesus was very clear about. On three occasions he describes

Satan in this way: in John 12.31, John 14.30 and John 16.11.

> 'Now is the judgment of this world, now shall the ruler of this world be cast out; and I, when I am lifted up from the earth, will draw all men to myself.'
> 'The ruler of this world is coming. He has no power over me; but I do as the Father has commanded me, so that the world may know that I love the Father.'
> 'When he' (the Holy Spirit) 'comes, he will convince the world of sin and of righteousness and of judgement; of sin, because they do not believe in me, of righteousness, because I go to the Father, and you will see me no more; of judgement, because the ruler of this world is judged.'

How come Jesus acknowledges Satan as the ruler of this world? If his only right to rule is that he deceived and stole the world then you would not expect Jesus to call him 'the prince of this world.'

The temptations shed further light on this in Luke 4.5-8:

> 'And the devil took him up, and showed him all the kingdoms of the world in a moment of time, and said to him, "To you I will give all this authority and their glory; for it has been delivered to me, and I give it to whom I will. If you, then, will worship me, it shall all be yours." And Jesus answered him, "It is written, 'You shall worship the Lord your God, and him only shall you serve'".'

Jesus did not contradict the devil's claim to authority: 'It has been delivered to me, and I give it to whom I will.' What he did contradict was his claim to the worship that only God deserves, 'It is written, "You shall worship the

Lord your God".' Satan so readily gets a hearing in human hearts and so easily embeds himself in the authority structures of the world because he has the spiritual right and authority to do so. This world is his legitimate sphere of spiritual operation. That is why he was in Eden in Genesis 3. What he should have been doing there was encouraging Eve to be fruitful and multiply, to have dominion over the earth and to take from the tree of life all the resources that she needed. He was an archangel of God, a mighty ministering spirit like Gabriel or Michael, hastening the work of the kingdom of heaven. But instead he chose to invent the reverse of heaven, wrested for himself the dominion that God wanted to share with all mankind in his love, and opened up instead the pit of hell. This is what Jesus means in Luke 10.18 when he says 'I saw Satan fall like lightning from heaven', and must therefore be the meaning of the passage he is quoting from Isaiah 14.12–15.

> 'How you are fallen from heaven, O Day Star, son of Dawn! How you are cut down to the ground, you who laid the nations low! You said in your heart, "I will ascend to heaven; above the stars of God I will set my throne on high; I will sit on the mount of assembly in the far north; I will ascend above the heights of the clouds, I will make myself like the Most High." But you are brought down to Sheol, to the depths of the Pit.'

It is not always easy to disentangle the Old Testament references to Satan from the world powers that so often become the embodiments of his kingdom and with which he clothes himself. However, understanding Jesus' teaching about Satan in this way at least helps explain why we would expect that to be the case, as well as making sense of difficult passages like Job 1 and Daniel 10. Satan goes to and fro on the earth because it is his proper sphere of operations. The princes of Persia and Greece are either Satanic personifications or lesser spirits under his authority. Clearly, when Satan fell, he moved from being an archangel to an archdemon and therefore carried many lesser angels with him in his rebellion, who now follow him in opposing the work of the kingdom of heaven. These latter are the unclean spirits or demons that Jesus contends with in the gospels and which we continue to be up against today. So, as well as the Holy Spirit and Satan, there are good spirits and bad spirits. The good spirits are angels and the bad ones are demons. This is perfectly clear if you compare Matthew 10.1 with Mark 3.15 and note that 'demons' and 'unclean spirits' are used interchangeably. Demons are unclean spirits. The writer to the Hebrews tells us in Hebrews 1.13–14 that angels are ministering spirits sent out from heaven to serve the saints. The word for 'spirit' in the Greek (*Pneuma*) is the same in each case. So angels and demons are spirits. Therefore we must be particularly careful to be in the Holy Spirit in this business of spiritual warfare so that we can always tell the difference between the two.

Satan's intentions are twofold. Ideally he wants to play God, but in his own way, which is the reverse of all that God is. His aim is for universal dominion based on pride, greed and selfishness. He wants to take over the lives, families, governments and worship of the world. To satiate his insatiable pride. To suck everything into a hell of his own making, which is the product of his proud heart. But at the same time he wants to destroy God and those who serve him, for the kingdom of God is an absolute threat to all his intentions.

God has provided three sets of relationships in the course of history in the context of which his kingdom can grow and mankind be protected from the Satanic kingdom. These are the family, the political authority and the church. This is seen clearly in the first three chapters of Matthew where chapter one locates Jesus in a family, chapter two in the context of the political authority and chapter three among the people of God. These also represent the main arenas of Satanic attack in the world. Both the family and the government come within the sphere of the kingdom of this world and the rule of Satan as the prince of this world. Both have been broken into by the fall of Satan and the subsequent fall of man. Sin universally leaves families open to the inroads and pressures of Satan and his demons. The authority of government is a peculiarly spiritual authority; that is to say, it transcends the individual lives and powers of those who govern and is invested in institutions, laws and traditions to which they are subject. It is exactly this sphere that is the area of Satan's legitimate power, given him as his realm of ministry before he fell. So government is his particular haunt and, taken together with the universality of sin, makes government an especially vulnerable arena for Satanic influence and further breakthrough into the lives of men and women.

The church, however, is God's special concern. Ever since the fall of Satan and the fall of man, God planned to open up his lamb-like heart to the world in such a way that man would turn back to him and let his mercy swallow up his sin. His plan was to begin again from within, by finding a man and a family that would receive his love and do his will. First there was Noah, then there was Abraham, to whom God promised in Genesis 12.3 'I will make of you a great nation . . . and in you all the families of the earth shall be blessed.' His purpose for the Jews was a people hidden in his own heart and protected by his own Spirit, to whom he could entrust his kingdom and through whom it could spread intact to all men and women who would receive it. Through such a people the Satanic kingdom could at the same time be destroyed from the earth, as with the Canaanites whose family and political life was so broken through and inhabited by the Satanic kingdom that its continued existence threatened to destroy the kingdom of love.

But instead, God's people gave way again to Satan. Instead of destroying the Canaanites, they took over their ways. 2 Kings 17.16 spells out the unthinkable:

> 'They forsook all the commandments of the Lord their God, and made for themselves molten images of two calves; and they made an Asherah, and worshipped all the host of heaven, and served Baal. And they burned their sons and their daughters as offerings, and used divination and sorcery.'

And when there was no one left to be the channel for the kingdom of God, the lamb of God stepped out of his own Father's heart and came to his broken people and began to gather them to himself and to give them his kingdom. For there was no other way if he was to have this kingdom, to share his heart with his people as he longed to do. And so Jesus came and the church was born. Providing a new family, the family of God, into which persons can be born again and grow in true value and freedom. A place where hurt people can be fathered and mothered, sistered and brothered into the wholeness that God uniquely intended them for when he designed them in the womb. Not destroying the old institution of family but providing a context in which it can be healed, renewed and protected as a channel for the life of God to flow through again. Providing a new alternative society in the earth, where

King Jesus reigns and his kingdom comes in power in the Holy Spirit – where the values of God can be taught and upheld in love; where the true objectives of corporate life, nurture and mission, can be planned and initiated. The city of God, salt and light, set on a hill in the world to open up the way to the kingdom of God, the New Jerusalem, that is coming. The church is not the kingdom, but the people to whom the kingdom is entrusted; not existing to destroy or take over the old society, the government and political authorities, but to be both the irritant and the preservative, the light and the challenge that keeps them to the pathway of justice and goodness, that gives the kingdom room to come.

Two things follow from all this. Firstly, it's not hard to see how the people in Jesus' day had come to be so badly demonised. They had lived in families which had given way repeatedly to selfishness and sin, where, instead of serving and loving one another in the image and way of God, personal desires and appetites were put first. People were treated like things. And as Satan's values were given way to more and more, so the demons took up residence. This is what Paul is talking about in Ephesians 2.1–2:

> 'And you he made alive, when you were dead in trespasses and sins in which you once walked, following the course of this world, following the prince of the power of the air, the spirit that is now at work in the sons of disobedience.'

Or else they have been opened up to terrible dishonour and ill treatment in the breakthrough of Satan and his demons into the political authority structures of the day. They had been oppressed, discriminated against, exploited, neglected and crushed until they gave way to spirits of rejection and self pity that now preyed permanently on them. Worst, and most unforgiveable, all this had been tragically exacerbated by the breakdown of the leadership of the people of God, through whom the people had been devastatingly exposed to Satan and his hosts, oppressed, exploited and neglected over generations by the very ones who should have been their shepherds and deliverers. It was all just as Ezekiel had prophesied in 34.2–5:

> 'Ho, shepherds of Israel who have been feeding yourselves! Should not shepherds feed the sheep? . . . The weak you have not strengthened, the sick you have not healed, the crippled you have not bound up, the strayed you have not brought back, the lost you have not sought, and with force and harshness you have ruled them. So they were scattered, because there was no shepherd; and they became food for the wild beasts.'

This was how the crowds had come to be so sick and demonised. They were sheep without a shepherd. Their rightful shepherds were now in Satan's kingdom, as Jesus said to the Jewish leaders in John 8.44, 'You are of your father the devil, and your will is to do your father's desires', and again in Matthew 23.29–33:

> 'Woe to you, scribes and Pharisees, hypocrites! for you build the tombs of the prophets and adorn the monuments of the righteous, saying "If we had lived in the days of our fathers, we would not have taken part with them in shedding the blood of the prophets." Thus you witness against yourselves, that you are sons of those who murdered the prophets. Fill up, then, the measure of your fathers. You serpents, you brood of vipers, how are you to escape being sentenced to hell?'

The second thing we can learn from this is that the church today is the absolute target for Satanic attack. If the church can be cracked, its leaders subverted and its people broken into, then the hordes of hell can come pouring in and the work of the kingdom hindered for generations. Yet this is exactly what has been happening again and again in the history of the church. It is absolutely vital that we understand the rock on which we are built and know our enemy and the frontiers and weapons of his attack. Otherwise, church history, even our own church history will leave us sick at heart, unbelieving and despairing. Having no real hope left of ever sharing the kingdom of God. This is exactly what Satan wants to happen, and is his greatest current success in the church today, if we are really honest. This is why spiritual warfare is so vital to our evangelism.

ii Getting down to battle

The greater our understanding of the battle for the kingdom of God, and the greater our insight into the background history of the people of God up until today, the greater our inclination is to weep. This was John the apostle's experience at the beginning of the revelation which God gave to him for the church. He was on the island of Patmos, fellowshipping with us in the kingdom of God, sandwiched between trouble and patient endurance. Almost certainly he was a prisoner there because of his fearless commitment to evangelism. During his time there he received disturbing news from the churches which were on his heart. But pressing on in the Spirit he had a glorious vision of the Lord. Then the Lord began to speak the truth about the churches, one by one. Continuing in the Spirit he saw right into heaven, to the throne, where the will of God issues from the heart of God. There in God's hand was a scroll, full up with the plans and purposes of God for his world and for his people. But it was sealed up, and no one was worthy to open it or to look into it. This is just our experience today when we begin to see as God sees. Then says John in Revelation 5.4, 'I wept much that no one was found worthy to open the scroll or to look into it.' He wasn't weeping before he saw into heaven, but when in fellowship with the Holy Spirit he saw into heaven then the compassion that fills heaven began to move him. That is how it needs to be with us. The greatest weapon against the pride of Satan and his kingdom is the compassion of Father. It was this that brought the Lamb of his heart into the world to destroy the devil and all his works, and this same love alone will finish the work that he came to do. But as we weep we need to understand that this is no merely emotional love, but a love so indestructibly strong that in Jesus, who is the son of that love, a stronghold has been established in the earth that shall never again be moved. John continues in Revelation 5.5–7:

> 'Then one of the elders said to me, "Weep not; lo, the Lion of the tribe of Judah, the Root of David, has conquered, so that he can open the scroll and its seven seals." And between the throne and the four living creatures and among the elders, I saw a Lamb standing, as though it had been slain, with seven norns and seven eyes, which are the seven spirits of God sent out into all the earth; and he went and took the scroll from the right hand of him who was seated on the throne.'

As we stop weeping and trust the victorious reigning lamb and his perfect sevenfold Spirit sent out into all the earth still, today, then the seals will begin to break and Jesus will ride out conquering and to conquer again and again. Jesus has defeated Satan. He is risen. His divine life is unstoppably ours if we will receive it. Paul says in Colossians 1.9–15:

> 'In him the whole fulness of deity dwells bodily, and you have come to fulness of life in him, who is the head of all rule and authority . . . you, who were dead in trespasses and the uncircumcision of your flesh, God made alive together with him, having forgiven us all our trespasses . . . he disarmed the principalities and powers and made a public example of them, triumphing over them in him.'

We have been given an indestructible Jesus and an indestructible kingdom. Jesus says in Luke 10.19: 'I have given you authority to tread upon serpents and scorpions, and over all the power of the enemy', and again in Matthew 16.18, 'And on this rock I will build my church, and the powers of death shall not prevail against it.' This kingdom of God that has been given us in the Holy Spirit cannot be shaken.

As we fellowship in the Holy Spirit, enjoying and thanking God for his kingdom, the Spirit himself will lead us out into warfare, just as he led the Lord Jesus. Matthew 3.16–4.1 tells us:

> 'When Jesus was baptised, he went up immediately from the water, and behold, the heavens were opened and he saw the Spirit of God descending like a dove, and alighting on him; and lo, a voice from heaven, saying, "This is my beloved Son, with whom I am well pleased." Then Jesus was led by the spirit into the wilderness to be tempted by the devil.'

What follows is a very crucial passage of Scripture: crucial because the way that Satan tempted Jesus is going to be fundamental to our understanding of Satan's strategy generally. To get to Jesus Satan will have used his deadliest tactics. We need to be wise to them.

Then, as now, Satan's weapons had one common aim and came from three specific directions. These three directions are particularly, but not exclusively, appropriate to the three arenas of his attack that we have already looked at: the individual in his or her family relationships, the established authorities and the people of God or the church. His aim is to lift up our hearts in pride to build a 'me-first kingdom' where what we want comes first. Simple basic immoral stuff this, which any child can understand, but which the more sophisticated tend to rationalise and cover over. The three directions from which the attacks come are our physical appetites (particularly strong on the home front), our social relations (particularly relevant on the social and political front) and our spiritual attitudes (particularly relevant among God's people). This may sound harmless enough, but in fact these areas are all embracing, touching the roots of our humanity, body, soul and spirit. So we need to investigate them very carefully.

The first attack on Jesus was the temptation to turn stones into bread:

> 'And the tempter came and said to him, "If you are the Son of God, command these stones to become loaves of bread." But he answered, "It is written, 'Man shall not live by bread alone, but by every word that proceeds from the mouth of God'".'

This temptation was quite simply to make getting bread more important than hearing from God. To use what power he had to feed his physical appetite instead of to hear from heaven. He was hungry, so it would not have been gluttony. Later he turns water into wine and multiplies bread and fish, so it would not have been a wrong action in principle. The wrong lay in the motive, which would have been 'my appetites and needs before God's word and God's world.' That doesn't even sound very bad, does it? That's because it is materialism, which is one of the basic values of the world – 'look after number one; if you don't look after yourself no one else will; it's backs to the wall, mate, may the best man win; I'm all right, Jack! look after your own class or people' and so on. But it is demonic nonetheless, a fundamental Satanic value. Give way to it, and the kingdom of hell moves a step nearer. Jesus came to feed the hungry, raise up the poor, bring in prosperity and feasting for ever, not by the way of selfish materialism but by God's way of loving and giving which comes to us by the Spirit as we listen and obey his living word above everything else. Of course this temptation could be expanded to include other appetites and physical needs; sex, sleep, possessions generally and so on. But the core issue remains the same.

The second and third attacks are recorded in the opposite order by Matthew and Luke. Satan has no particular system. If he can get us off guard he will. The second attack in Luke 4.5–8 is one we have already looked at on page 58, and shows Satan's real power over the authority structures of this world. The temptation here is to desire and choose authority over other people and their families, lives, and possessions for one's own glory, instead of choosing to worship God and serve his interests and therefore his kingdom. It's important to notice here that to choose authority and glory for your own sake is equivalent to worshipping Satan. So the choice and exercise of authority for 'own' glory instead of 'God's glory' is a second fundamental Satanic value. Once again, it is so normal, so much a part of the way the world functions that it's difficult to grasp how totally wrong footed it is. But there's no question about it. The disciples found difficulty in grasping this too. Even at the last supper they were disputing about their personal positions. In Luke 22.25–27 Jesus answered them like this:

> 'The kings of the Gentiles exercise lordship over them; and those in authority over them are called benefactors. But not so with you; rather let the greatest among you become as the youngest, and the leader as one who serves. For which is the greater, one who sits at table, or one who serves? Is it not the one who sits at table? But I am among you as one who serves.'

This is a very basic matter, from our closest relationships with friends and family right out through school, work, government and so on. The domination and manipulation of others for our own ends sets up the perfect environment for demon activity because it actually constitutes the worship of Satan. It is a complete copy of the way he operates.

The third attack in Luke 4.9–12 took Jesus to the highest point of the temple:

> 'And he took him to Jerusalem, and set him on the pinnacle of the temple, and said to him, "If you are the Son of God, throw yourself down from here; for it is written, 'He will give his angels charge of you, to guard you', and 'On their hands they will bear you up, lest you strike your foot against a stone'." And Jesus answered him, "It is said, 'You shall not tempt the Lord your God'."'

This temptation was God-competition. That is to say it was the temptation to compete with God; to be the one who called the tune for God. It is really the most fundamental of all the temptations. With it Satan invited Jesus to take the highest place and to expect God to serve him in so doing. To have done so would not only have been to usurp God's place, but actually to make him the opposite kind of God to the one he is. For the point is that God *does* exist to serve me, he is such a loving humble God. That is why he made the promise of protection in Psalm 91 that Satan quoted. But that promise is made for those who cling closely to him in love, knowing his name and character, and wanting to be like him. And to be like him is not to reach for the highest place, but the lowest. Isaiah 57.15 quotes God directly:

> 'For thus says the high and lofty one who inhabits eternity, whose name is Holy: "I dwell in the high and holy place and also with him who is of a contrite and humble spirit."'

To seek to climb up over, and be exalted in the eyes of others is to seek the hellish kingdom that Satan has formed. It is dreadfully significant that it is to the pinnacle of the temple that Satan took Jesus for this temptation. This is still Satan's commonest angle of attack to get in among the people of God. Selfish ambition is, as we have already seen in chapter two, lethal to the kingdom of God. Even to moan and groan among ourselves about how hard done by we are in the work of the kingdom, or to complain to God that he is not making things easy for us, when his whole heart is to bless us and win this fight over his enemies, is a dreadful slight on God's character. It was just this kind of attitude at Massah in the wilderness that first provoked Moses to ask in Exodus 17.2, 'Why do you put the Lord your God to the test?' This kind of wrong attitude to God destroyed the work of the kingdom throughout the whole history of the northern kingdom of Israel where they worshipped Jehovah as a Baal, a god of appeasement who would bless you if you were nice to him. Such a god is in Satan's image. God is love, and he exists to bless. We don't have to be nice to him for him to bless us. We simply have to receive him, and that means that we change to his image and not he to ours.

All this is of course, like the rest of Jesus' responses to the temptations, quite upside down in comparison with the values of the world. But this is just what Isaiah was getting at when he quoted the Lord, in Isaiah 55.9:

> 'For my thoughts are not your thoughts, neither are your ways my ways, says the Lord. For as the heavens are higher than the earth, so are my ways than your ways and my thoughts than your thoughts.'

Jesus came to bring heaven to earth and Satan couldn't stop him. The subtlety of these three attacks of Satan, if we give way to them, is that they apparently take us higher and higher and further and further in our satisfaction and dominion over our whole world, whereas actually what Satan is doing is penetrating us internally right to the heart; body (have what you want to have: bread first), soul (be who you want to be: glorious in power) and spirit (expect God to serve your ends: the highest place for number one). Finally, if we give way on these altogether, then we simply become outposts, vassals of Satan's kingdom. We become just like him.

(iii) Moving into attack

These prongs of attack which we have seen in Jesus' temptations are both our internal and external battle fronts in spiritual warfare. In the work of evangelism we often get to points where the way seems to be blocked in front of us. We are seeking to move ahead in obedience to the Holy Spirit, we are engaged in spiritual warfare, and yet we are making no inroads on the enemy. The sick are not healed, the demons won't go and people are not getting converted. If we are not knowingly sinning, if we are listening to God, then he will show us that there are further internal frontiers of spiritual warfare to be taken for him. These internal issues will be related to one or another of these spiritual battle fronts, where somehow the fundamental Satanic values have seared our spirits. We will need forgiving, healing or delivering from them. In some cases we may need literal deliverance from them in the sense that we have so given in to them or been oppressed by others with them that we have become prey to actual demons. Then we will need help to get free, we will need to turn to others with whom we share fellowship in the Spirit. On each occasion that I have experienced this, I have also known a parallel breakthrough in spiritual power in the ministry of the kingdom. This is not to suggest that we turn inwards and go digging internally: rather that as we progress in the work then the Spirit will show us when new breakthrough is required on the internal front as well. But we must give ourselves to develop a real sensitivity to, and hatred for, these Satanic values, so that we are able to recognise them and either oppose them or protect ourselves from them as the case may be. All the powers of the demonic kingdom are arrayed behind these frontiers in the attempt to break into our personal lives and families, into society and above all, into the church, for surely the demons follow their master. As God's people we should be aware of and repudiate occult practices: yet they are only the by-products of the demonic strongholds represented by these three temptations. How much more we should hate and repudiate *them*.

In order to speak, pray and act against these Satanic

strongholds, we need to see, spiritually, deep down in our hearts, that Jesus really has overcome them and that Satan actually is a defeated enemy. Fortunately it is an easy task to trace the interplay between Jesus and these strongholds through his ministry and to the cosmic confrontation at the Cross where, as Paul puts it in Colossians 2.15, 'He disarmed the principalities and powers and made a public example of them, triumphing over them.'

At the end of the temptations Luke 4.13 records, 'When the devil had ended every temptation, he departed from him until an opportune time.' On many occasions during his ministry Jesus faced these same attacks again, and each time he triumphed. Put positively, Jesus' responses to the devil's temptations were to put the living word before his own physical needs, to worship and serve instead of seeking to be served, and to take the lowest place instead of using God to get status. Jesus constantly lived this way. For example, when Jesus came to Jacob's well at Sychar John tells us in 4.6–7 that he was weary and clearly implies that he was also hungry and thirsty.

> 'Jesus, wearied as he was with his journey, sat down beside the well. It was about the sixth hour. There came a woman of Samaria to draw water. Jesus said to her, "Give me a drink", for his disciples had gone away into the city to buy food.'

He was so concerned to value the woman and bring the good news of eternal life to her that not only is it never recorded that he got the drink he asked for, but by the time the disciples returned he was too busy sharing the good news even to have time to eat!

> 'The woman left her water jar, and went away into

> the city, and said to the people, "Come, see a man who told me all that ever I did. Can this be the Christ?" They went out of the city and were coming to him. Meanwhile the disciples besought him, saying, "Rabbi, eat." But he said to them, "I have food to eat of which you do not know . . . My food is to do the will of him who sent me, and to accomplish his work." '

Word not bread.

Later, after Jesus fed the five thousand, (because when you put the living word first you begin to discover how to release bread to the hungry) the crowds wanted to make him their king. John 6.15 tells us, 'Perceiving then that they were about to come and take him by force to make him king, Jesus withdrew again to the hills by himself.' Worship not dominion.

Another time it was the feast of Tabernacles and Jesus was staying behind in Judea because the Jewish leaders were threatening to kill him. But his brothers wanted him to go and show off his works publicly at the feast. Jesus said to them in John 7.6–9:

> ' "My time has not yet come, but your time is always here. The world cannot hate you, but it hates me because I testify of it that its works are evil. Go to the feast yourselves: I am not going up to this feast; for my time has not yet fully come". So saying he remained in Galilee.'

Humility not a public show of power.

The failure of Israel's leaders had been so total by the time Jesus came that the Satanic strongholds dominated the lives of the people from the leaders downwards. Ultimately it was quite simply the lust for money, the lust for power and the lust for position, evidence of those same three strongholds which we have been tracing, which were behind the specific sins which put Jesus on the cross. But the stream of God's compassion continued to pour out unstemmed.

Judas betrayed him for money. But as he hung dying Jesus wouldn't even take the drug they offered him, because he wanted to fulfil the truth about God to the very end and carry away every last effect of selfish materialism. He thirsted for us and so his love penetrated the heart of the hardened thief who lives to see his kingdom! 'And he said, "Jesus, remember me when you come in your kingly power." And he said to him, "Truly, I say to you, today you will be with me in Paradise" '. Jesus broke the dominion of materialism and the lust for bread.

Pilate allowed him to be crucified for political expediency, because he realised that he would gain the most power from the situation that way. But in the full knowledge that Pilate had no power over him unless it was given to him from above, Jesus refused to appeal to his Father for twelve legions of angels or more which Matthew 26.53 tells us he would have sent at once, because he was determined to worship and serve his Father against all the effects of the dominion and glory of Pilate, Rome and every self-centred use of authority. He kept his spirit for his Father to the very end and so his love penetrated the heart of the very centurion who had presided over his crucifixion. 'Now when the centurion saw what had taken place, he praised God, and said, "Certainly this man was innocent!" ' and ' "Truly this man was the Son of God!" ' Jesus broke the dominion of imperialism and the lust for power over others.

Caiaphas had Jesus condemned to death because he was a threat to his position as High Priest, because he wanted to keep the highest place in the temple for himself, whereas Jesus had prophesied its complete downfall. But even in the ultimate extremity of the cross Jesus never yielded to the temptation to fall back on the Father's promise of protection, despite all the taunts of the passers-by that if he was the Son of God he should come down from the cross. He proved the nature of his Father's loving authority by humbling himself and taking the lowest place, the pit of God-forsakenness that pride has opened up. And so too his love penetrated the hearts of rich Joseph of Arimathea and the Pharisee Nicodemus who had feared the loss of status and position because of their secret discipleship, and they came out in public and asked for his body. Jesus broke the dominion of selfish ambition and the lust for position over others.

In Jesus the fundamental principalities and powers have been broken. They can no longer shake his kingdom. On this rock he is building his church and the gates of hell cannot prevail against it. We have this unshakeable, unstoppable kingdom in the Holy Spirit. But, as the writer to the Hebrews has it in Hebrews 2.8, 'We do not yet see everything in subjection to him.' So what are we to do to see his kingdom come in our day? In the verses that follow, the writer to the Hebrews exhorts us to consider Jesus, to take care not to have hard and unbelieving hearts, to strive for the present reality of the kingdom, to hold fast our public confession of faith in Jesus and finally to pray with confidence, fully expecting to receive mercy and find grace to help us.

It is this culmination of confidence in prayer which is at the heart of spiritual warfare. This confidence in the kingdom of Jesus is so great that it is a place of rest, but not a passive or inactive rest. It is reached through the exertion of genuine faith. It is a rest that we strive (Heb. 4.11 lit: hurry) to enter and a confession which we hold fast (Heb. 4.14 lit: take hold of mightily, powerfully). This is why it involves fasting and praise, and is not just an individual matter but requires the help and support of others. Clearly Jesus prayed both alone and together with his disciples. Luke tells us in Luke 5.16 that 'he withdrew to the wilderness and prayed'; in Luke 6.12, 'he went out into the hills to pray; and all night he continued in prayer to God' and in Luke 9.18, 'he was praying alone.' But Luke also records those times when Jesus prayed with his disciples as in Luke 9.28: 'he took with him Peter and John and James, and went up onto the mountain to pray' and again in Luke 11.1: 'he was praying in a certain place, and when he ceased, one of his disciples said to him, "Lord, teach us to pray . . .".' We need to discover and maintain a balanced interplay between private and corporate prayer. My experience has been that it requires a meeting of individuals who have broken through in the private internal frontiers of the spiritual battle, for corporate prayer to break through the external frontiers of the enemy's kingdom and advance the kingdom of God. On the other hand, the internal battle for the kingdom within is rarely successful without the eventual help of corporate prayer with trusted brothers and sisters. Both are essential aspects of spiritual warfare which we now need to look at in more detail.

As we have already noted from Hebrews chapter two, it is confident prayer that brings present success for God's kingdom. But this is precisely what we so often lack and so the progress of the kingdom is held up. A couple of years ago some of us were struggling to see breakthrough in one of the many inner city estates in which we are involved in planting churches. God told us that the way ahead would be through supernatural healings. But pray as I did for various sick people there, the expected healings and breakthrough were not coming. Reaching out for a word of knowledge to illuminate one woman's need, the Lord gave me a word for myself instead, and by it revealed a level of fear and unbelief that was hindering the passage of the Spirit through my life. John's words in 1 John 5.14 spoke to me. 'This is the confidence which we have in him, if we ask anything according to his will he hears us.' I knew that this was precisely the confidence which at that moment I didn't have. The problem was how to get it. I had discovered a new personal internal frontier in which I had to break through before we could move forward together in the external work. The Spirit showed me similar words of Jesus in John 15.7: 'If you abide in me, and my words abide in you, ask whatever you will, and it shall be done for you.' I was abiding in the Lord as fully as I knew how, but as I asked for revelation I realised immediately that there were a number of things that God had told me to do in the past, which as yet I'd not done. In that respect his words were not living in me. So I set myself to fast and pray until those matters were obeyed and settled in me. Some days I fasted entirely, some only partially – from butter and sugar or second helpings. The whole thing was a private battle until it neared the end, and even then I only shared it with a few who were particularly close to me. I only mention it now because it illustrates the kind of personal warfare we need to be ready for again and again. At the end the Lord brought to my mind a number of areas of hurt and spiritual damage which were hindering me. Then I needed the help, prayer and channel of my brothers' and sisters' lives for the Lord to get me free and heal me. Then I was able to move on strongly in the work God had given me to do. The great advantage of fasting is that when it is done in the right way it asserts the primacy of the spirit over the flesh and gets the whole human being functioning properly as a channel for the Spirit of God and therefore for the coming in of the kingdom of God. In this way fasting is a powerful spiritual exercise which keeps a person, or better still a whole body of people, spiritually fit. It was basic to Jesus' life, and needs to be to ours. The older manuscripts of Mark's gospel give us an important insight on this in the case of the demon possessed boy that the disciples had been unable to help. When the disciples ask why they had been unable to break through the unbelief of their generation and see the kingdom breaking in to the family concerned, Jesus said, In Mark 9.29 'This kind cannot be driven out by anything but prayer and fasting.' There is no evidence or even time for Jesus to have prayed and fasted at that point. It was the life style, the build up, of spiritual vitality that provided the channel for the Holy Spirit to operate. Some people have mistakenly thought that Jesus' remarks in Mark 2.18–20 about wedding guests not needing to fast while the bridegroom is present meant that neither Jesus nor his disciples fasted. Far from it. The point Jesus makes is that he is bringing in the kingdom in the present, so the ethos is joy and celebration, not mourning and fasting, apart from the gloom and darkness of the Cross when the bridegroom is taken away. But the kind of fasting that gets hold of the kingdom and makes a way for the Holy Spirit to overcome God's enemies is a different matter. This is what Jesus is referring to in Matthew 6.16–18:

> 'When you fast, do not look dismal, like the hypocrites, for they disfigure their faces that their fasting may be seen by men. Truly I say to you, they have their reward. But when you fast, anoint your head and wash your face, that your fasting may not be seen by men but by your Father who is in secret; and your Father who sees in secret will reward you.'

The twin dangers with fasting are the hypocrisy which trusts in the fasting, not in God, and the legalism which brings us into the wrong ethos of asceticism and defeatism and forgets the triumphalism of a kingdom given us in the present in the Holy Spirit. But fasting with prayer and praise in the ongoing battle context of serving the world with the words, works and warnings of the Father's compassionate heart is great power. When we develop this habit of maintaining spiritual fitness, God is able to use us in breaking through against the attacks and temptations that otherwise will destroy the lives of those we are trying to help. The Lord allows us at times, as priests and intercessors on their behalf, to face and overcome the temptations that they give way to, and even the demons that they then fall prey to, so that we can be the channel of Christ's deliverance to them, so that they can get really free and receive him.

James tells us in 5.14–16:

> 'Is any among you sick? let him call for the elders of the church, and let them pray over him, anointing him with oil in the name of the Lord; and the prayer of faith will save the sick man, and the Lord will raise him up . . . The prayer of a righteous man has great power in its effects.'

The prayer is corporate, but those praying are individuals whose prayers will have great power if they are righteous. We have been exploring the way that Christ's righteousness gets deeper into our lives so that our prayers and work for him become much more effective. When a whole fellowship of people moves together in this way, great gains can be made for the kingdom of God. We have discovered a little of this together in Ichthus, but the potential for the people of God to shift the enemy from his entrenched positions in churches, governments, families and individuals is enormously greater than we are yet getting hold of in our day. May God help us. As Paul puts it in 2 Corinthians 10.3–4, 'For though we live in the world we are not carrying on a worldly war, for the weapons of our warfare are not worldly but have divine power to destroy strongholds.'

I have referred to some earlier experiences of spiritual warfare at the beginning of this chapter. It was during the difficult final weeks of setting up the student movement in the South Pacific that one desperate night I discovered very powerfully the truth of Jesus' words in Matthew 18.19: 'Again I say to you, if two of you agree on earth about anything they ask, it will be done for them by my Father in heaven.' There was one student leader I absolutely had to contact in the space of about ten minutes. The future of the work virtually depended on it. Nobody knew where he was in the whole campus. Those words dropped, I think, for the first meaningful time, into my head. I grabbed a passing Christian. 'Will you pray with me in agreement on this? Amen.' We opened our eyes and there he was!

I have already mentioned experiences in corporate prayer during student missions. These days we are finding that regular periods of what we call praise-warfare – times of high praise, of identifying key issues in the past and present of a place and its people, of agreeing together on the will of God in the matter – break open hard inner city areas to the good news and many people come to Christ. The leaders of a church near here were praying in this kind of way in an attempt to overcome a real blockage to worship they experienced in a particular building. One of them received a specific word of knowledge that the root of the problem was an evil religious spirit with roots back into the year 1912.

Corporately they agreed together and commanded the spirit to leave. As a result there was a dramatic improvement in their worship. Later research showed that a healing and revival crusade had taken place nearby in that year. A meeting of the church had discredited it and thrown out a number of members who had been healed and baptised in the Spirit at the crusade. Obviously the Holy Spirit had been grieved and place given to demons. But spiritual warfare took back the ground gained by the enemy.

In several particularly strategic prayer times for some of our Lewisham congregations the Lord showed us a number of demonic forces at work in the borough. In particular these included a spirit of broken heartedness or grief, a spirit of unjust trade and a spirit of isolation. Ongoing research has uncovered many of the roots of these. South East London suffered devastatingly in the Second World War. One hundred and sixty flying bombs fell, one in fourteen homes were destroyed, and the worst bomb disaster of the war was right in the middle of Lewisham town centre. We have subsequently discovered that many whose spiritual wisdom we respect had independently recognised a spirit of unjust trade as a key principality over London. Only five years ago the centre of the borough was torn by class and race rioting. Since we have named and begun to wage spiritual war on these powers we have seen greater break throughs in signs and wonders, healings and above all receptivity to the good news even in the open air meetings in the town centre which had previously been pretty tough. There is a very long way to go, but we are on the way now.

Some people are doubtful, even cynical about this kind of warfare. It is certainly Biblical. When it is waged in the context of the ongoing good news of the kingdom in words, works and warnings, it is both practical and successful. It was how Jesus carried on in such undeniable power against Satan that his opponents could only protest that it was Satan's own power he was using. He replied in Matthew 12.28–29:

> 'But if it is by the Spirit of God that I cast out demons, then the kingdom of God has come upon you. Or how can one enter a strong man's house and plunder his goods, unless he first binds the strong man? Then indeed he may plunder his house.'

It was how the early Christians carried on in the face of the same opposition and persecution that killed Jesus. In Acts 4 when Peter and John were released, the early Christians straightaway lifted their voices together in prayer and insisted, as Jesus had insisted, on the predetermined hand and plan of God. And that was no passive fatalistic will of God but nothing less than the kingdom of Jesus breaking through against the strongholds of materialism and power lust and status seeking embodied, as we have already seen, in the human powers of their day.

> 'For truly in this city there were gathered together against thy holy servant Jesus, whom thou didst anoint, both Herod and Pontius Pilate, with the Gentiles and the peoples of Israel, to do whatever thy hand and thy plan had predestined to take place. And now Lord, look upon their threats, and grant to thy servants to speak thy word with all boldness, while thou stretchest out thy hand to heal, and signs and wonders are performed through the name of thy holy servant Jesus. And when they had prayed, the place in which they were gathered together was shaken; and they were all filled with the Holy Spirit and spoke the

> word of God with boldness . . . And with great power the apostles gave their testimony to the resurrection of the Lord Jesus, and great grace was upon them all.'

It is out of this kind of warfare today that our words of good news will come with great power, our works of compassion erupt into signs and wonders and our warnings change the face of the ruling authorities and make room for the kingdom of our Lord Jesus that is coming.

Chapter 4

Kingdom Words

(i) Words as a part of the whole good news

(a) Words and works belong together

God and everything that he has made are inextricably linked to words. God has never been silent, without word. It is his nature to speak, to reveal himself, to make himself known. This is the simple and primary meaning of John 1.1: 'In the beginning was the Word, and the Word was with God, and the Word was God.'

From the very start, God's word brought action. In Genesis 1.3: 'God said, "Let there be light"; and there was light.' Throughout the whole creation story God spoke the word and it was done.

God's words are never empty. They bring action into the world. Or to put it another way, they are incarnated. Throughout Old Testament history this was true. God told Noah that there would be a flood; there was a flood. He told Abraham that he would have a son; he had a son. He told Moses he would deliver the Israelites from Egypt; he delivered them from Egypt. His words always issued in action and the actions, like the words, revealed the character of God. He was judge, saviour, deliverer and so on. When God was ready to reveal himself completely, then Jesus came. As John 1.14 puts it, 'The Word became flesh and dwelt among us, full of grace and truth; we have beheld his glory, glory as of the only Son from the Father.' It was not only the words that Jesus said that revealed the Father's glory, but the works that he did. This was so thoroughly true that Jesus could say in John 14.10, 'The words that I say to you I do not speak on my own authority; but the Father who dwells in me does his works.' We might have expected Jesus to have said either 'the works that I do I don't do on my own authority . . .' or else 'but the Father who dwells in me speaks his words'. But he mixes the two, the words and the works. It was all *together* the word. So it must be with us. The good news, is what Jesus said and did. Our good news, our evangelism, consists of what we say and do.

This partnership of word and action in the Bible, coming as it does to its culmination in Jesus, the word made flesh, means that for us to emphasise words alone, without the action, is at best meaningless and at worst false, disproved on the spot and giving the lie to our message. From a Biblical viewpoint the current debates over whether words are more important to evangelism than works, that put Evangelism and Social Action in order of importance or even in opposition to each other, or relegate signs and wonders to the early church age, are very silly. Words and works together make up the good news. Both are seriously weakened, if not falsified, if they are separated. Jesus and the disciples never separated them. The words Jesus used always drew attention to the works he was doing. The words explained the works or the works demonstrated the truth of the words. This is implicit in the introduction to his ministry in Mark 1.15: 'Jesus came into Galilee, preaching the gospel of God, and saying, "The time is fulfilled, and the kingdom of God is at hand; repent, and believe in the gospel".' Already in chapter one we saw that the statement 'the kingdom of God is at hand' or 'nearby' drew people's attention to Jesus himself. Almost straightaway he went into the synagogue at Capernaum and began to teach. Mark 1.22 tells us 'They were astonished at his teaching, for he taught them as one who had authority, and not as the scribes.' A man with an unclean spirit immediately began to cry out, and Jesus rebuked the spirit and delivered the man. The crowds had no difficulty in grasping that what he did was part of what he said.

> 'And they were all amazed, so that they questioned among themselves saying, "What is this? A new teaching! With authority he commands even the unclean spirits, and they obey him." '

In the beginning of Jesus' ministry in Luke's gospel the connection of word and work is completely explicit. In the synagogue in Nazareth Jesus declared:

> 'The Spirit of the Lord is upon me, because he has anointed me to preach the good news to the poor. He has sent me to proclaim release to the captives and recovering of sight to the blind, to set at liberty those who are oppressed . . .' (Luke 4.18)

His preaching and his proclamation did just that. The captives went free and the blind saw! What he said and what he did were one message.

In the book of Acts there is a very strong emphasis on the fact that the apostles preached the cross and the resurrection. Some people have tried to suggest that this proves that preaching the word is more important than doing the works of the gospel. But of course it really proves the exact opposite. The cross and the resurrection are at the heart of the gospel precisely because words alone are not enough. It was not enough for Jesus to describe the Father's heart, his mercy, his willingness to forgive and share his life with us. It was not even sufficient for Jesus to demonstrate the Father's heart as he went about doing good. The supremacy of love over hate, of life over death, of the Holy Spirit over Satan, of mercy over judgement, of the kingdom of God over the kingdom of this world, this had not only to be proclaimed and demonstrated, it had to be *achieved*, the ultimate battle had to take place and be won. This is what happened at the cross. Now there is no effect of what Satan or sin can do against God and his world, against me or other people, that is too great to be overcome by the resurrection power of God, through the cross and in the Holy Spirit. This is why the early Christians preached the cross and the resurrection. The lamb-like heart of God had always been the motivation of God's dealings with his people and his world. It was the source of all that Jesus revealed. The roots of the cross and the resurrection had always been there in the nature of God, at the throne of his kingdom. But now the Father's heart had been revealed in the face of the worst and most implacable opposition and had won through it all. Now the Cross and resurrection had not only been prophesied, but actualised! So the early Christians did not *only* preach the cross and resurrection. They preached and lived the kingdom way of life that Jesus lived and that the cross and resurrection secured forever. And they demonstrated its power by the things they said and the things they did. Their gospel, like Jesus' gospel, was good news in words and actions. Peter's first sermon preached the life of Jesus as well as his death and resurrection in an attempt to explain the Holy Spirit's actions at Pentecost. His second sermon concentrated mainly on the death and resurrection but was sparked off by the dramatic healing of the lame man in the name of Jesus. The third sermon at Cornelius' house in Caesarea emphasised Jesus' life and work equally with his cross and resurrection at an event which would never have happened without the action of the Holy Spirit in speaking to both Peter and Cornelius in visions, and was itself a demonstration of the gospel that in Jesus there is neither Jew nor Greek.

From the very beginning the context in which people were becoming Christians every day was one in which the word was preached, taught and talked while at the same time signs and wonders were done and neighbour love practised. Luke tells us in Acts 2.40–47:

> 'And he testified with many other words and exhorted them, saying, "Save yourselves from this crooked generation . . ." And many wonders and signs were done through the apostles . . . and they sold their possessions and goods and distributed them to all, as any had need.'

Massive church growth took place when 'preaching the word' and 'serving tables' were done together. Luke describes in Acts 6 the way in which social action had become such a large part of the good news that it was in danger of squeezing out the preaching of the word altogether. When the balance was put right again, we read in Acts 6.7, 'And the word of God increased; and the number of the disciples multiplied greatly in Jerusalem.' World evangelism was born in a context where preaching and teaching took place alongside the relief of famine. The massive numerical growth in Jerusalem gave rise to persecution which scattered the Christians. Luke tells us in Acts 2 that those who came to Antioch preached the Lord

Jesus there to Jew and Gentile alike. Barnabas was sent down from Jerusalem by the apostles to help in the work and he went and brought Saul from Tarsus with him. The Holy Spirit foretold a world famine and so the disciples determined to send Barnabas and Paul on a mission back to Jerusalem with supplies to relieve the famine. As the famine was to be world wide it seems safe to assume that the relief was being sent to Jerusalem as a central place for distribution. The disciples were first called Christians at this time.

Far from tailing off because they were no longer a centrally significant part of the gospel, as some have bizarrely suggested, these supernatural signs and wonders and acts of practical neighbour love continued throughout New Testament days as a fundamental part of evangelism. On Paul's final journey to Rome, while shipwrecked on Malta, Luke tells us in Acts 28.8–9:

> 'In the neighbourhood of that place were lands belonging to the chief man of the island, named Publius, who received us and entertained us hospitably for three days. It happened that the father of Publius lay sick with fever and dysentery; and Paul visited him and prayed, and putting his hands on him healed him. And when this had taken place, the rest of the people on the island who had diseases also came and were cured.'

When writing to the Galatians Paul reminds them of how Peter, James and John, had given their unconditional blessing to his mission to the Gentiles in Galatians 2.8–10: 'except they would have us remember the poor, which very thing I was eager to do.' It should be clear, I think, that the words and the works of Jesus are all part of the good news!

Paul puts it like this in 2 Corinthians 4.5: 'For what we preach is not ourselves, but Jesus Christ as Lord, with ourselves as your servants for Jesus' sake.' Not only is this Biblical evangelism but it is the kind of evangelism we need if we are going to overcome the contemporary crisis of confidence in words, and the disillusionment with answers, that is so endemic in the inner cities of today. We are often asked why Ichthus Christian Fellowship has grown so fast numerically over the years. Actually we are anticipating much greater growth and are not at all content with what we have seen so far. Nevertheless I am convinced that the cutting edge to our evangelism has been provided by the combination of words and works which has given an integrity to our message and earned us a serious hearing. Both the development of our Jesus Action programme in an attempt to meet the practical needs of our neighbourhoods and the growing experience of signs and wonders which have been taking place among us, have been a crucial part of our evangelism, without which many of our words would have been wasted.

(b) Word and Spirit belong together

Just as the words and works of the gospel are inseparable, the same is true of the word and the Spirit. Jesus always spoke in the power of the Spirit. Words alone are not enough. As Jesus put it in John 6.63, 'It is the spirit that gives life, the flesh is of no avail; the words that I have spoken to you are spirit and life.' This is the key to the partnership of word and work in evangelism. Words spoken in the Spirit have the same potential power that they had at the beginning in Genesis 1.2–3 when 'The Spirit of God was moving over the face of the waters. And God said, "Let there be light"; and there was light.' This was how Jesus spoke such words and did such works as he promised to do in Luke 4.18: 'The Spirit of the Lord is upon me, because he has anointed me to preach good news to the poor. He has sent me to proclaim release to the captives and recovering of sight to the blind.' And this in turn was how Paul evangelised with such great effect as he described to the Thessalonians in 1 Thessalonians 1.5: 'For our gospel came to you not only in word, but also in power and in the Holy Spirit and with full conviction.'

One dreadful result of, or perhaps reason for, the unnatural separation of the words and the works of the gospel is that a rift has occurred between the word and the Spirit. If words can stand alone without obvious effects or demonstrations, then it is possible for words to masquerade as the good news when they are no such thing. This is what happened to the Pharisees of Jesus' day. Jesus said of them in John 5.37 that they had never heard the Father's voice despite the fact that they searched the scriptures and claimed to be his spokesmen.

> 'The Father who sent me has himself borne witness to me. His voice you have never heard, his form you have never seen; and you do not have his word abiding in you, for you do not believe him who he has sent. You search the scriptures, because you think that in them you have eternal life; and it is they that bear witness to me; yet you refuse to come to me that you may have life.'

They searched the scriptures, but they never heard the voice of God. They thought that the scriptures had life in themselves. But only as we react spiritually to the scriptures do we hear the voice of God and receive his living word. The scriptures bear witness, but without our receptivity to the Holy Spirit they cannot speak to us. As a result, the

Pharisees, said Jesus in Matthew 15.6–9, taught doctrines, based on scripture texts, which actually made the word of God empty and were destructive and dishonouring to those who they were responsible for.

> 'For the sake of your tradition, you have made void the word of God. You hypocrites! Well did Isaiah prophesy of you, when he said: "This people honours me with their lips, but their heart is far from me; in vain do they worship me, teaching as doctrines the precepts of men." '

This is tough stuff, but it shows that the words of scripture themselves operate at a dual level; a verbal one and a spiritual one. A person needs to hear and to communicate on both levels to preach the word of God. This is what Paul is getting at when he tells the Corinthians in 2 Corinthians 2.6: 'The written code kills, but the Spirit gives life.' The written code was never intended to kill, but rather to witness to Jesus, but unless the communicators are themselves operating in the Holy Spirit, the word becomes a destructive thing. Now if this is even true of the scriptures, how much more is this true of our own words as we speak out the good news. We need to be sure that the words we speak are like King David's words in 2 Samuel 23.2: 'The Spirit of the Lord speaks by me, his word is upon my tongue.'

As far back as I can remember I have been aware of a fundamental distinction between some preachers and teachers of the word and others. With some you hear from heaven and meet the Lord, with others you do not. And some of the ones who do bring the Lord bring him more than others. It has nothing to do with verbal eloquence, with simply being a 'good speaker'. Some 'good speakers' have a negative effect in retrospect. They make you feel condemned. One quite famous preacher nearly always ended up making one friend of mine backslide. Nor is it entirely a matter of content either, although it is related to it. It is all a question of spirit. Some are like the Pharisees who used the scripture in a destructive way, whereas others are like Stephen of whom it is said in Acts 6.10: 'They could not withstand the wisdom and the Spirit with which he spoke.'

Now not everyone will be called to preach and teach God's word publicly. But Jesus did not only preach and teach, he also talked the gospel. Every member of the body can do this. But this too requires a spiritual ministry. The task and responsibility of ministering the word with the Spirit is for everyone. Since the living word of God is spiritual and not just verbal, it is communicated by our spirit and not only by our minds and tongues. Therefore the spiritual condition of the witnesses becomes a fundamental matter in the ongoing task of evangelism. Here we can see how spiritual warfare relates to the communication of the word. Of course the battle context means that the demons will try to snatch away the word we preach. Jesus made that clear in the parable of the sower in Matthew 13.19: 'When any one hears the word of the kingdom and does not understand it, the evil one comes and snatches away what is sown along the path.' But how stupid if the word is not understood because we fail to communicate it with the Holy Spirit. Our own internal battle for strength and cleanness of spirit is vital here. I shared something of my own personal experience of this in the last chapter. The most noticeable breakthroughs in my own communication of the word, such as it is, have been the result of that. Paul speaks in his second letter to the Corinthians about ministering God's word in the kind of way that brings word and Spirit together with power. In order to do this he says, it is crucial to open our hearts more deeply so that the Holy Spirit can deal with any hardness that remains there. Hardness of heart is caused by pride that refuses to acknowledge the need for more of God or by defilements of body and spirit that we harden our hearts to cover, rather as a scab forms over a wound to protect the sensitive area. Such defilements can be caused by our own sin or by other people's. We need to open up our hearts and let the Holy Spirit deal with the damage. Then, says Paul in 2 Corinthians 4.5–6, we can minister God's word with the same creative power that was released when God said 'let light shine out of darkness' back in the beginning.

> 'For what we preach is not ourselves, but Jesus Christ as Lord, with ourselves as your servants for Jesus' sake. For it is the God who said, "let light shine out of darkness", who has shone in our hearts to give the light of the knowledge of the glory of God in the face of Christ.'

When we open up our hearts more to the Spirit in this way, it is the Lord Jesus to whom we open up. For as Paul puts it in 2 Corinthians 3.17, 'the Lord is the Spirit.' Clearly then, the best way to minister the word with the Spirit is to minister Jesus. The content of our message needs to be him, all the time. This is the part played by the spoken word in evangelism. We speak about Jesus in the Spirit of Jesus. We describe Jesus with our words, we demonstrate Jesus by our works, we convey the Spirit of Jesus through our spirits. The word is incarnated again in and through our lives, and the kingdom of God draws near.

(ii) The particular role of the spoken word in spreading the good news

(a) The spoken word and the scriptures

Today then, the word is still incarnated in Jesus, in and through us, his body, by the Holy Spirit, in warfare, words and works. This is all evangelism. However, the spoken word does have a particular part to play. Words are the special vehicle and gift through which revelation and knowledge of God comes. They are the image, in man, of our wonderful personal God's ability and desire to communicate and share his love with another. Our ability to understand and speak words derives from Jesus, the ultimate word who spoke us into being in the first place. Now that the ultimate word has been made flesh and lived among us, our words have become the ideal vehicle for communicating *the* word, our Lord Jesus.

Before Jesus came in the flesh he was already speaking. He spoke by the world he had created, through which, as Paul puts it in Romans 1.20: 'his eternal power and deity' can be 'clearly perceived'. He spoke through men and women made in God's image, whose lives, despite their sinfulness, still mirrored something of his fatherhood and his tender mother heart. So we can understand what it means when he says in Jeremiah 31.9, 'For I am a father of Israel' and in Isaiah 49.15, 'Can a woman forget her sucking child, that she have no compassion on the son of her womb? Even these may forget, yet I will not forget you.'

But he spoke especially, by the Spirit, through the written words of the prophets, whose sometimes humble, open and available lives gave God the opportunity to speak into the world and so prepare the way for his full revelation in the coming of the living word, the word made flesh, Jesus himself. As the writer puts it in Hebrews 1.1–3:

> 'In many and various ways God spoke of old to our fathers by the prophets; but in these last days he has spoken to us by a Son, whom he appointed heir of all things, through whom also he created the world. He reflects the glory of God and bears the very stamp of his nature, upholding the universe by the word of his power.'

It is hardly surprising then, that when Jesus spoke he used words soaked in the inspired words of the scriptures that prepared the way for him. In the same way, if we are to be faithful to his commission to us, we must speak words soaked in the same scriptures, interpreted now through the lens of the Lord Jesus himself and the gospels, together with the rest of the inspired writings of those who became his faithful witnesses as he had promised. But if we are to speak like this, we need to discover more of the way in which Jesus understood and used scripture so that we can do the same.

Three things stand out about Jesus' use of the scriptures; the way he saw himself in them all, the progressive way he interpreted the law and the substitutionary way he applied the prophets. I've written already in chapter one of the crucial insights gained by putting Jesus, and therefore the gospels, first in all our Biblical interpretation. This method is firmly rooted in Jesus' own use of the scriptures, for he saw himself in all of them, and interpreted them accordingly. Luke puts it very succinctly as he describes the incident on the Emmaus Road in Luke 24.27. 'And beginning with Moses and all the prophets, he interpreted to them in all the scriptures the things concerning himself.' The emphasis on the word 'all', as in 'all the prophets' and 'all the scriptures' really underlines the point here. Jesus is to be found in all the books of the Bible and in all parts of those books. Later in the same chapter Luke emphasises the need for Jesus to open their minds to understand the scriptures, and again in John 5.39 Jesus exposes the failure of the Jews to find life in the scriptures because of their failure to come to him in order to understand them.

This Jesus-centred way of using scripture wonderfully expands the scope and power of our preaching of Jesus and hence of the whole of the good news of the kingdom. This is exactly Paul's point when he reminds Timothy in 2 Timothy 3.15–16:

> 'From childhood you have been acquainted with the sacred writings which are able to instruct you for salvation through faith in Christ Jesus. All scripture is inspired by God and profitable for teaching, for reproof, for correction, and for training in righteousness.'

That is to say, all scripture is inspired by God and able to instruct us for salvation, *through faith in Christ Jesus*. All scripture, if we find Jesus there, opens up a living situation in which the kingdom can be revealed. If we open up the scriptures correctly, whether it be in personal conversation, a one-to-one Bible study, a home group or a large evangelistic or teaching meeting, then Jesus will step right out into that situation and reveal himself and his kingdom by the Spirit. But if we do not find Jesus there, then our opinion or explanation of God's word can condemn, mislead and damage people spiritually. Jesus blames the Pharisees and scribes for just this in Matthew 15.1–9. By placing together the scriptures that command honour for parents and those that command the giving of tithes and offerings, they concluded that the letter of the law excused them from giving financial support to their parents. Jesus said:

> 'So, for the sake of your tradition, you have made void

> the word of God. You hypocrites! Well did Isaiah prophesy of you, when he said: "This people honours me with their lips, but their hearts are far from me; in vain do they worship me, teaching as doctrines the precepts of men." '

This kind of exegesis has continued down the years and has been consistently devaluing and damaging especially to those in disadvantaged situations. It was used to justify slavery less than 150 years ago, and continues in many places today to be used to dishonour and prevent women from playing their proper part in the ministry and leadership of the church and society. Of course it is not always damaging in such overt ways but nonetheless generally has the effect of putting people down. Jesus, on the other hand wonderfully raised people up into a greater vision and experience of the heavenly Father's perfect kingdom as he expounded the scriptures. This is especially obvious in his use of the law during the Sermon on the Mount in Matthew 5.

Instead of applying the letter of the law Jesus applied the law in a progressive way. That is to say he interpreted the law in the light of his own loving and merciful heart and lifestyle. In this way he shed God's light on its original intention and meaning. As Jesus quoted in Matthew 5.38:

> 'You have heard that it was said, "An eye for an eye and a tooth for a tooth". But I say to you, Do not resist one who is evil. But if anyone strikes you on the right cheek, turn to him the other also.'

Now at superficial face value Jesus flatly contradicts the law here. However, if we take Jesus as the point of interpretation then we understand the law. 'An eye for an eye and a tooth for a tooth' was not a law of vengeance and retribution but a law of progression towards the perfect law of the Father's kingdom of love. It had carried the Jews away from reacting to violence with escalating vengeance, towards mercy and love for their enemies. Now Jesus had come to take them all the way to its conclusion. This way of interpreting the law, we must understand, is Jesus' way, and far from weakening it, affirms it in its entirety forever. For as Jesus says in the same sermon in Matthew 5.17–20:

> 'Think not that I have come to abolish the law and the prophets; I have not come to abolish them but to fulfil them. For truly, I say to you, till heaven and earth pass away, not an iota, not a dot, will pass from the law until all is accomplished. Whoever then relaxes one of the least of these commandments and teaches men so, shall be called least in the kingdom of heaven; but he who does them and teaches them shall be called great in the kingdom of heaven. For I tell you, unless your righteousness exceeds that of the scribes and Pharisees, you will never enter the kingdom of heaven.'

So to interpret Biblical truth in this progressive kind of way, by faith in Jesus, is to fulfil its every dot and iota, whereas to apply it literally and legalistically to people and situations is to relax it and risk blocking the way into the kingdom for both them and us. This is dreadfully serious. To suggest, as some do, that in order to preach the gospel it is first necessary to preach the Old Testament law, without first preaching Christ, is quite wrong. It is denigrating to Jesus and unfaithful to his gospel. The law is fulfilled in Jesus and so is to be declared keepable by those who receive him and not to be used to condemn people. To use the law in that way is simply unchristian. As Jesus said to Nicodemus in John 3.17:

> 'For God sent the Son into the world, not to condemn the world, but that the world might be saved through him. He who believes in him is not condemned, he who does not believe is condemned already, because he has not believed in the name of the only Son of God.'

The incident of the woman taken in adultery in John 8.1–12 contrasts perfectly the right and wrong ways of using the law. The Pharisees applied it literally and legalistically to condemn the woman, and at the same time, therefore, Jesus. 'Teacher, this woman has been caught in the act of adultery. Now in the law Moses commanded us to stone such. What do you say about her?' Jesus brought his own light on the subject. As he said afterwards: 'I am the light of the world; he who follows me will not walk in darkness, but will have the light of life.'

He interpreted the law progressively. He was after all the law maker, writing again on the ground with his finger, as God had written the law on tablets of stone. But he was the fulfilment of the purposes of the Jewish nation, proclaiming the ultimate restoration, the consummation of God's purpose for Israel. He marked the end of the age in which the Jews had special responsibility to reveal the faithfulness of God's heart. To witness God's utterly faithful and pure love for mankind they had to be so strong on sin that adulteresses had to be stoned. But now the age that God had chosen the Jews to prepare the way for had dawned. The age of his love and compassion for all mankind, the kingdom of God, had begun in Jesus. If the woman would repent and sin no more there was mercy for her as for all mankind.

The progressive way of interpreting scripture is particularly exciting when it is applied to the teaching of the prophets. They all addressed themselves to the failure of Israel to keep the law and were a constant reminder to the people of God of their destiny to be God's covenant people. They prophesied God's judgement on Israel, but at the same time spoke in terms of God's forgiveness and restoration which would come to the remnant that repented and was faithful to God. These promises of restoration predicted a wonderful future for a repentant Israel. Joel's prophecy in Joel 3.18–21 is one among many:

> 'And in that day the mountains shall drip with sweet wine, and the hills shall flow with milk, and all the stream beds of Judah shall flow with water; and a fountain shall come forth from the house of the Lord and water the valley of Shittim. Egypt shall become a desolation and Edom a desolate wilderness, for the violence done to the people of Judah, because they have shed innocent blood in their land. But Judah shall be inhabited forever, and Jerusalem to all generations.'

Some prophets went further still, and remembered that God's original intention for Israel was that she should be a channel of his blessing to all mankind. Amos and Zechariah spoke not only of blessing for Israel but of similar blessing for the remnant of her enemies, for Edom and the Philistines. Micah spoke of such a future for the remnant of Israel:

> 'It shall come to pass in the latter days that the mountain of the house of the Lord shall be established as the highest of the mountains, and shall be raised up

> above the hills; and peoples shall flow to it, and many nations shall come, and say: "Come, let us go up to the mountain of the Lord, to the house of the God of Jacob; that he may teach us his ways and we may walk in his paths" . . . and they shall beat their swords into ploughshares, and their spears into pruning hooks; nation shall not lift up sword against nation, neither shall they learn war any more.'

Jesus interpreted *all* this as fulfilled in him. He simply substituted, swapped himself for the condemned Israel, under God's judgement together with the rest of mankind that God had intended Israel to bring to repentance. This, he saw, totally fulfilled the prophets, who spoke as in Isaiah 53, of God doing exactly this by means of his suffering servant, like a sacrificial lamb 'wounded for our transgressions . . . bruised for our iniquities; upon him was the chastisement that made us whole, and with his stripes we are healed.'

As Jesus put it, in his own words before the cross in Luke 22.37, 'For I tell you that this scripture must be fulfilled in me, "And he was reckoned with the transgressors"; for what is written about me has its fulfilment.'

Or like Zechariah, who spoke in chapter 13.6–7 of the shepherd who would be struck down in his own house and among his own people, which Jesus applied to himself in Matthew 26.31: 'You will all fall away because of me this night; for it is written, "I will strike the shepherd, and the sheep of the flock will be scattered". But after I am raised up, I will go before you to Galilee.'

Jesus did not only see himself as the substitute for the judgement prophesied for the people of Israel, but also as the substitute, the swap for the promised future kingdom and destiny of Israel. As Hosea put it in 6.1–3:

> 'Come, let us return to the Lord; for he has torn, that he may heal us; he has stricken, and he will bind us up. After two days he will revive us; on the third day he will raise us up, that we may live before him. Let us know, let us press on to know the Lord; his going forth is sure as the dawn; he will come to us as the showers, as the spring rains that water the earth.'

Jesus applied all the prophecies of Israel's future destiny and kingdom to himself and took the kingdom for himself and his remnant of repentant followers in all the earth. He applied the wonderful prophecy of Zechariah 9.9–10 to himself by riding into Jerusalem on an ass.

> 'Rejoice greatly, O daughter of Zion! Shout aloud, O daughter of Jerusalem! lo your king comes to you; triumphant and victorious is he, humble and riding on an ass, on a colt the foal of an ass. I will cut off the chariot from Ephraim and the war horse from Jerusalem; and the battle bow shall be cut off, and he shall command peace to the nations; his dominion shall be from sea to sea, and from the River to the ends of the earth.'

He *gave* this glorious kingdom to his little bunch of followers in Luke 12.32: 'Fear not, little flock, for it is your Father's good pleasure to give you the kingdom.' He *took the kingdom away* from the old Israel and gave it his new alternative nation, the church, in Matthew 21.42–43:

> 'Jesus said to them, "Have you never read the scriptures: The very stone that the builders rejected has become the head of the corner; this was the Lord's doing, and it is marvellous in our eyes?

> Therefore I tell you, the kingdom of God will be taken away from you and given to a nation producing the fruits of it." '

He made this kingdom available for all the world in Matthew 24.14 and 28.19 when he said to his disciples:

> '. . . this gospel of the kingdom will be preached throughout the whole world, as a testimony to all nations; and then the end will come . . . Go therefore and make disciples of all nations, baptising them in the name of the Father and of the Son and of the Holy Spirit, teaching them to observe all that I have commanded you; and lo, I am with you always, to the close of the age.'

Now all this has enormous implications for our verbal witness to Jesus. For not only do we have all the aspects of the kingdom of God in the gospels to draw on. Nor do we simply have the explanations and applications of the kingdom in the rest of the New Testament to add to them. But as the New Testament writers so well understood, the whole Old Testament Israel experience is ours to draw from in explaining and applying the gospel today. We can warn from their failures, but always in the light of God's wonderful substitutionary mercy towards us in Jesus and we can share now in their promised destiny, receiving as much of the eternal kingdom as we can get hold of from the Lord Jesus in the Holy Spirit. For as Paul puts it to the Galatians in 3.13–14:

> 'Christ redeemed us from the curse of the law, having become a curse for us – for it is written, "Cursed be every one who hangs on a tree" – that in Christ Jesus

the blessing of Abraham might come upon the Gentiles, that we might receive the promise of the Spirit through faith.'

(b) The main types of verbal evangelism

Four particular ways of using the spoken word stand out in Jesus' ministry. He preached or heralded the good news, he taught the people, he rebuked and denounced the enemies of his kingdom, and he simply talked to people about who he was and the kingdom that he had come to bring. These give us a basic lead in our approaches today.

Two Greek words are translated as 'preaching' or 'heralding' the good news in the gospels. Sometimes they are also translated as 'announcing' or 'proclaiming'. The words are *'evangelizo'* which literally means to bring or announce good news, from which our word 'evangelism' derives and *'kerusso'*, which means to be a herald or to proclaim, from which the theologians' word kerygma derives. Strictly applied, this type of speaking refers to a slightly narrower approach than the one we normally describe as preaching today. Our word for preaching also includes part of what the gospels describe as teaching the good news. This need not be a problem as long as we retain the particular aspect of preaching that Jesus used so much. His kind of preaching denotes fairly short, intense and to the point declarations of the kingdom along the lines of a news communication of the impending visit of an important official, or the declaration of war or peace and so on. This kind of preaching will lead on to situations more suited to teaching and explaining the good news in greater depth. But it is a first essential for making a breakthrough, gaining a hearing and beginning a relationship in the Spirit. Jesus and the disciples preached like this from town to village, in the open air, at peoples' work places and in their homes. The beginning of Jesus' ministry is a good example of this. The impact of his public proclamation of the kingdom in Galilee in Mark 1.15 really excites the imagination when you see it in context. 'The time is fulfilled, and the kingdom of God is at hand; repent and believe the gospel.' At a time when Israel already had two kingdoms to contend with, Herod's and Caesar's, news of the intervention of God's kingdom was guaranteed to grip people's attention, as Jesus spoke out in the power of the Holy Spirit. Within a matter of days he had called Peter, Andrew, James, John and Matthew from their work places, held an overflowing home meeting and begun itinerating throughout the neighbouring towns and villages preaching both in synagogues and in the open air. It is our task today to so preach the kingdom that we have something of the same impact. This is not as hard as it used to seem. The old days of dry and unproductive evangelism disappear with the growth of the kind of fellowship in the Holy Spirit and spiritual warfare we have discussed in chapters two and three. When evangelism is of the whole kind which includes the context of works and the warnings of the gospel, which we have yet to explore more thoroughly in the concluding chapters, ears and hearts begin to open.

Mick (not his real name) is a man in his fifties. Brought up in care, he only returned to his father and step-mother as an adult, and spent the best part of his later life nursing them both. His step-mother died and since then he has been looking after Dad most of the time. A few weeks ago a team of us were holding an open air meeting in the courtyard of the council estate where he lives. He came out onto the balcony to see what was going on. We were preaching the gospel something like this:

> 'God has visited London in a special way a good number of times in its history. It's happening again

> these days. It's about time. We need it. This is why we are celebrating. He loves you and has got wonderful plans for us together whoever you are. He calls it his kingdom. Don't miss out on it. Jesus helps us understand about it. Come and share with us tonight at the local centre.'

We put a leaflet through his door that said something similar. He came that night, and again several times. He opened up to Christ. He said afterwards 'I've never been so happy in all my life.' Now he is part of the local community of Christians.

Cynthia (again not her real name) had worked among down and outs until she was attacked one night. Now her own son had ended up on the streets, breaking up through drugs and alcohol. Her own spirit began to break and she lost her health and her job. She hadn't been outside her house for a year. A couple of local Christians called at her door. Their approach was not religious or argumentative, saying that she had to believe this or that. It was caring, pastoral. True evangelism is really pastoral work. Caring for the lost sheep! They preached the good news of the kingdom to her, it went something as follows:

> 'God's Spirit is moving again in London. Jesus can still mend broken hearts, broken homes, broken communities. Why don't you come to a home meeting up the road tomorrow and meet some local Christian friends who have found this to be true?'

She came the next morning to the home meeting, and again in the evening. She was surprised to find that there was hardly room to get everybody in the door. She felt at home. The Christians prayed for her and anointed her with oil for healing on the way home in the car. Two nights later she was at a public meeting . . . now she is discovering that you can really trust Jesus, and belongs to a newly planted local group of believers. And so I could go on. The key ingredients are the good news of the kingdom preached in an immediately incisive and relevant way, in the power of the Spirit and with genuine active love.

These days we don't generally associate the teacher with evangelism. But a great deal of Jesus' teaching was in that context. Preaching gets the attention of the hearer, but the good news generally needs more explaining than a preach can provide. Preaching gets the person, the audience, the interest; teaching follows. Jesus taught in the synagogue if they gave him the opportunity, he taught crowds in the open air, he taught small groups in homes or in transit and he taught on a one-to-one basis. He taught people as soon as they were willing to give time and attention to hear, whether they were his committed followers yet or not. He went on teaching his disciples about the kingdom right up until the day that he was taken up. We have found all four of these types of teaching situation extremely fruitful for contemporary evangelism and ongoing teaching.

The first is the local worship situation provided by the synagogue in Jesus' day, and in some cases still in the early church days in Acts. This had the advantage of being local, and of providing continuity with God's past activities in the area. It also had distinct disadvantages, such as the legalistic approach to religion and the limited and inadequate expression given to the nature of the kingdom in the structure of existing services. There was no scope for women, children or gentiles! There were ways past this, however, such as deliberately introducing radical kingdom teaching, purposely doing away with unhelpful or anti-kingdom restrictions or moving to a convenient hall nearby!

Joking apart, the former was exactly what Jesus did in Nazareth by raising the issue of Naaman the Syrian and the widow from Zarephath and in other places by repeatedly healing on the Sabbath day. The latter was exactly what Paul eventually did at Ephesus. Neither acted in a fleshly, unloving way in advance of the Spirit of course, although, I suspect the Jews weren't too convinced about that.

This kind of local situation in which teaching can be given in a community context is ideal as a starting point for evangelistic teaching, either in the context of a church based mission, or of a church planting project. An informal event where as broad a cross section as possible of the local social, cultural, and age groups are made to feel at home, in a way expressive of the kingdom, is an excellent situation for teaching it. We have used barn dances, gospel cabarets, family nights and theme orientated presentations of music and drama on many occasions to good effect. In each case something between ten and forty minutes of direct teaching can be given, depending on the composition of the group and the degree of interest that has been stimulated before the event by the preaching of the good news. In most cases where young children are involved it is best to provide an alternative activity for them during the teaching time. Often a brief period of worship celebration helps provide a platform for the teaching, as long as it is explained properly and new folk are encouraged to participate or spectate as they wish. This kind of community situation in a local area makes an equally ideal environment for regular ongoing worship and teaching while at the same time providing an excellent meeting point into which to bring new converts or inquirers. We have found that this is currently the best form of Sunday morning get together for the church at which with good use of visual aids, something like twenty minutes of simple but no less fundamental and spiritual teaching can be given to a wide cross section of believers and inquirers. Where use is being made of an existing Christian community of some years standing for this kind of meeting, the parallel with the synagogue is of course very relevant. I would not recommend taking this on unless very clearly invited to do so, as past tradition definitely does have to give way to a valid contemporary expression of the kingdom. This involves at the very least the participation of people and the moving of furniture which law and tradition may well tend to prohibit. So we need to have spiritual sensitivity and aggressive courage like Jesus!

The large scale area event has a different but no less important part to play. Jesus taught the crowds on the mountain, on the plain and by the lakeside. There the emphasis was less on community and more on the sense of mass movement. This kind of situation provides an excellent opportunity to bring a prophetic word from heaven, in which people get a real sense of history and the momentum of God's work in it, and in which they are being caught up. Of course this kind of event requires teaching, and therefore a teacher, of maturity and wisdom, but it had a vital part to play in Jesus' ministry and still has today. Such an event puts the good news of the kingdom in perspective and mobilises people into action for God. The market place sermons and Solomon's Porch meetings in the early church life in Acts were of this kind. We are familiar with them these days in the context of area or citywide evangelism, and as such they have a strategic part to play in getting people moving into the kingdom. But as more and more people are getting converted and mobilised, regular teaching meetings of this sort maintain vision and momentum. They can be held on a monthly or even a weekly basis to great effect. This has certainly been our experience within Ichthus over the last few years. Once again the combination of worship celebration and teaching is best as it establishes an atmosphere where God is at home and in which the hearts of the people are open to what he has to say.

It has been a sad fact throughout the history of the church that one or another crucial part of the church's calling and lifestyle has been either neglected, or emphasised to the detriment of another part. This has often been the case with different types of teaching. Some churches opt for the big event, and people travel in from all around, others for the local event, and still others for the small group. But all have an important part to play. This is so clear from the teaching of Jesus that it is probably sinister that we have so often missed it! We need to realise that God cares for all kinds of people and that he can build us together into his community in our own locality. We need to realise that he is the God of history and the whole world and that he is on the move on a large scale to bring all men and women to him. We also need to know that he cares for us individually and personally and has a unique part for us to play in his body. This is where teaching in the small group situation comes in. The two great advantages of small group situations is that they are geared to individual participation and face-to-face relationships. This is exactly the involvement that God invites us into with himself, and wants to build us into together. Without this the larger meetings will fail to be alive with his Spirit. For God not only speaks to and encounters us vertically in relationship to him, but horizontally in relationship to each other. Nor does God intend to mediate his life to us via others, but through the instrument of preachers and teachers to bring us into a relationship with him together, in which, as Jeremiah prophesies in 31.34:

> 'No longer shall each man teach his neighbour and each his brother, saying "Know the Lord", for they shall all know me, from the least of them to the greatest, says the Lord.'

Probably the two most famous group teaching situations in Jesus' ministry are the discussion on the road to Caesarea Philippi and the Last Supper. But careful reading of the gospels reveals that the disciples formed a small group discussion around Jesus which continued for three years! Such is the effectiveness of the beginners' group and home group these days that we have found them similarly difficult to break up at times! In the evangelistic situation of church mission or planting the small group is the best context for teaching beginners. It allows them to interact with the gospel by interruptions, questions and their own insights. The group leader needs to develop Jesus' skills of using non directive questions ('Who do men say that the Son of man is?') or making provocative statements which get a positive response from the group ('Where I am going you cannot follow me now') which can then be used as a peg or a step to move the discussion forward. The gospels themselves make the obvious basis for discussion. This is what they were written for!

Small groups are probably best held in someone's home. If they need to be held somewhere else a sense of homeliness and togetherness needs to be maintained as far as possible. We have found that the beginners' group needs to be run only for a few times at first, so that the commitment required is not too off-putting for the inquirer. Later a new group can be started which runs for several months. In the long term the small group is also the ideal unit for pastoral care, and teaching becomes one element among several. But the same principles of participation and personal relationship in study apply. Where group discussion is unsuitable, such as with the use of video and tapes, time can still be set aside for questions and discussion afterwards to get the best out of the small group environment.

The fourth way that Jesus taught people was on a one-to-one basis. In some cases, such as with the woman at the well the situation grew out of conversation; others, like with Nicodemus were less informal. The one-to-one situation is specially suited to getting people going in the Christian life. Whatever form of evangelism is the means whereby a person comes to Christ some element of one-to-one teaching is the necessary requirement for getting them moving with the best possible start. Getting born generally requires a midwife. So does getting born again. These days post natal clinics safeguard the health of our babies by regular check ups. The one-to-one can have a similar function! The great advantage of one-to-one teaching is that it can be entirely geared to the individual needs of the person concerned. The gospels, as ever, are the best place to start talking. The method is particularly suited to people with special needs, the new Christian, the person with particular hurts and problems to get through, the teenager adjusting to the transition from childhood to adulthood and so on.

One way in which Jesus spoke out the good news of the kingdom that is largely misunderstood, misapplied or ignored, is the way he spoke out against evil. This takes us beyond Jesus' use of words and into a further area of the content of kingdom evangelism, which we will investigate under the heading of 'kingdom warnings' in the final chapter. However, we need to touch on it here because it involves a way of speaking that is strictly neither preaching, teaching or talking good news. At face value it is bad news, and as such might not seem part of the gospel of the kingdom at all. But it must be, because Jesus went in for it. There is one recurrent word and one recurrent phrase typically used to introduce this kind of speaking in the gospels. These are the word 'rebuke' and the phrase 'woe to you' which is a way of denouncing somebody. This kind of speaking is part of the good news simply because evangelism is more than just good news. It is good news to the poor, both physically and spiritually. When the sources of poverty are spoken against, when the evil powers of this age are attacked, then it is very good news to the poor indeed!

Jesus' practice of speaking against evil is directly related to the issue of spiritual warfare which we have already discussed. Where the power of the enemy was represented by evil spirits, in disease, or in antagonism via the weather, he spoke a direct word of rebuke. For example, he rebuked Peter's mother-in-law's fever, he rebuked the wind and the waves several times and often rebuked the demons. We need to realise that exactly the same forces are against us today as we move out in the work of the kingdom, and it is all part of the good news that we oppose them with the same aggression that the Lord used and see them overcome as he did. This obviously requires wisdom in the Holy Spirit, but so does the rest of evangelism.

As we saw in the previous chapter, the powers of Satan are particularly arrayed against us in terms of materialism, power lust and status seeking. These powers embodied themselves in Jesus' day in the establishment elites, in particular the Pharisees, Sadducees, chief priests and scribes, as well as in Herod's and Pilate's courts. Jesus himself took the initiative in exposing and denouncing this fact, as well as countering their evil attitudes and actions with his truth. He did not always speak out, he relied on the Spirit to show him his Father's will. Nevertheless in

Matthew's gospel alone, he spoke out on eleven separate occasions, denouncing their behaviour on thirty-five separate issues! Among other things he specifically and publicly accused them of being children of hell, neglecting justice, mercy and faith, full of extortion and greed, whitewashed tombs full of dead men's bones, sons of murderers, hard hearted, serpents, wretches and teachers of dangerously contaminating doctrines.

Whenever today the established leaders of government, commerce, education or the church are guilty of any of these same things that their counterparts of Jesus' day were, then we must be wide open to his method of exposing them. This is part of the rôle of the spoken word in evangelism. We need to be led by the Spirit and to have a whole lot of wisdom in this area, because obviously it can get us a load of flack and we may end up in prison or even killed, and we don't want that to happen unnecessarily! We shall deal with this whole area thoroughly in the final chapter. It was because Jesus was so aware of the dangers involved in this side of his evangelism that he occasionally used the word for rebuke in its alternative sense in the Greek of 'warn' or 'sternly charge'. He at times warned both people whom he had healed and his disciples not to make the fact known straight away, simply because he wanted to finish the rest of the work he had come to do before the authorities stopped him. As we move into this side of evangelism we may have to keep people from unwisely talking and prejudicing our work in this way too.

Jesus did a great deal of talking. He wasn't always preaching, teaching or denouncing evil. He simply talked the good news to people. A big gospel like his was relevant to everything, so there was always something worth saying. This is still true. Once we get a big enough gospel the problem is not so much how to start talking but to know when to stop. What stands out about Jesus' conversations with people is that although he was God, the Word, the Truth, he really knew how to listen, how to use his conversation to communicate the fundamental kingdom values of love, relationship and the worth of persons. There are many examples of Jesus' conversations in the gospels, among the most outstanding are the ones with the woman at the well, Nicodemus, the rich young ruler and Zacchaeus. Each one a shining example of the way Jesus loved and honoured people despite the sin which he had come to save them from. Again and again I find myself going back to John 4 and the woman at the well. I'm so glad the Holy Spirit brought that one back to John's mind! It is so rich with illumination for us in our talking for the kingdom. The living holy God asks this outcast sinful woman for a drink! What a brilliant start. How much more should we value and honour people. How ever did he avoid a heavy patronising answer to her question about his lack of sexism and racism? But, instead, just the humble, fundamental metaphor of the living water. And what economy of words and patient confidence in the woman's ability to grasp the spiritual significance of kingdom truth! Then that uncomplicated injection of supernatural insight: 'Go call your husband and come here.' That took faith and courage. Then the immensely positive answer to the apparent red herring, really only an attempt on her part to buy time and learn more all at once. It would have been so easy to get bogged down in the theology of that one. And finally the humility and personal risk with which he opened his heart and revealed himself to her – the first person in the world to know unequivocally from his own testimony who Jesus was.

Just a few hours ago I was interrupted in writing by a young man who came to see me. Just a few hassles, he said, that he wanted to talk through, thought I might be able to help. What a privilege to be trusted. I was so aware even as he arrived, of the need to put him at his ease, be on the same level together, give him his worth. So many of the problems I had talked over with countless other people before him. What a temptation to cut in too soon, to ask the obvious question glibly or banally. What a blessing to know Jesus love and desire to listen, to find just the right word to speak of him. To see the Spirit touching, helping, changing a man again. What a God and friend Jesus is. He doesn't keep his love or his skill to himself. Now you and I pass them on too!

Chapter 5

Kingdom Works

(i) The works of the kingdom and the work of the cross

The works of the kingdom were mainly of three kinds in Jesus' ministry: healing, casting out demons and liberating the poor. A great deal of his ministry was taken up with these, and he commissioned both his disciples and us to do the same. This is the point of Matthew 9.35–10.1:

> 'Jesus went about all the cities and villages, teaching in their synagogues and preaching the gospel of the kingdom, and healing every disease and every infirmity. When he saw the crowds, he had compassion for them, because they were harassed and helpless, like sheep without a shepherd. Then he said to his disciples, "The harvest is plentiful, but the labourers are few; pray therefore the lord of the harvest to send out labourers into his harvest." And he called to him his twelve disciples and gave them authority over unclean spirits, to cast them out, and to heal every disease and every infirmity.'

While John the Baptist was in prison he wanted reassuring that he had been right in all he had said about Jesus and sent his disciples to Jesus for confirmation that he really was the

Messiah come to bring in the age of God. Jesus answered, in Matthew 11.4–6:

> 'Go and tell John what you hear and see: the blind receive their sight and the lame walk, lepers are cleansed and the deaf hear, and the dead are raised up, and the poor have good news preached to them. And blessed is he who takes no offence at me.'

This is kingdom evangelism.

There are two other works which Jesus did only once or twice, but characterised his kingdom in a fundamental way. He fed the crowds and he washed his disciples' feet. Both these events had an underlying spiritual significance which it is very important to get hold of. For they illustrate the primacy of the Spirit and the necessity of God's compassion in our works of the kingdom. The feeding of the four and five thousands definitely prove that God cares about the hungry and that it is his heart to feed them. But at the same time Jesus emphasises in his explanation of the feeding of the five thousand in John 6.63, 'It is the spirit that gives life, the flesh is of no avail'.

Not that the physical is unimportant or of no vital concern to God, but that spiritual life is the key to solving the physical problems and not vice versa. There is no kingdom way of meeting the physical needs of the world without first feeding on Jesus.

The foot washing incident proves that when all around you people are giving way to the Satanic powers of materialism, power lust and status seeking, as the disciples at the last supper were doing, the only kingdom way to counter attack is by strong practical loving. For behind all Jesus' works of the kingdom lay the compassion of God's great heart, seen in the climax of Jesus' ministry in the

Cross and resurrection; the greatest work of them all. There, as we considered in detail in chapter 3, Jesus took on all the root causes of sickness, demon activity, dishonour and oppression. With his own flesh and blood he wiped the dirt and disease of sin and guilt away from the world for all who will receive it. With his own spirit he reaches out now to bathe us and feed us. That is the unique work of Jesus, that we cannot do, for it is finished and done once for all. In Isaiah's words in Isaiah 53.4–5:

> 'Surely he has borne our griefs and carried our sorrows; yet we esteemed him stricken, smitten by God, and afflicted. But he was wounded for our transgressions, he was bruised for our iniquities; upon him was the chastisement that made us whole, and with his stripes we are healed.'

For us who have received all this, the work of the kingdom is to speak and demonstrate what Jesus has done to secure his kingdom for ever. We show it by works motivated by the same compassion that took Jesus to the cross. Works which are by their very nature the proof and reality of the power of the cross. Without it there would be no true healing, no deliverance, no honour for the poor.

(ii) The works of the kingdom and the Holy Spirit

The kingdom of God is in the Holy Spirit. This is the crunch point, and one at which some Christians part company. For not everything that seems to be a good work is a work of the kingdom. Jesus came to heal the sick, cast out devils and liberate the poor. But always by the works of the Holy Spirit and never by the works of the flesh. Paul states very clearly in Galatians 5.19:

> 'Now the works of the flesh are plain; immorality, impurity, licentiousness, idolatry, sorcery, enmity, strife, jealousy, anger, selfishness, party spirit, envy, drunkenness, carousing and the like. I warn you, as I warned you before, that those who do such things shall not inherit the kingdom of God.'

Nothing that includes sorcery, enmity, strife, jealousy, anger, selfishness, dissension, party spirit or envy is by any stretch of the imagination a work of the kingdom of God. This is not to say that no one who gets involved in any of these things can ever do anything good or sincere, nor that the parties, churches or organisations they work for are totally depraved or devoid of sensible or relatively just policies. All men and women are after all made in God's image, however fallen. Simply that we should never confuse their actions with the works of the kingdom of God. Jesus said, in Matthew 7.20, 'You shall know them by their fruits', and the fruit of the Spirit, Paul continues in Galatians 4.22, 'is love, joy, peace, patience, kindness, goodness, faithfulness, gentleness, self-control.' Without these qualities of the life of the Lord Jesus, he said that we could do nothing at all. As Paul sums it up in Romans 14.17 AV 'For the kingdom of God is not meat and drink; but righteousness, and peace, and joy in the Holy Spirit.' That is to say the kingdom of God is given to no one except those who have been spiritually reborn and are learning to live in the Spirit, under the same conditions of fellowship as those explored in chapter two. As Jesus says in Luke 12.32, 'Fear not, little flock, for it is your Father's good pleasure to give you the kingdom.' It is they who are its custodians for the world. They are the ones whom Jesus commissions to carry its good news by words and works into all the world. This is the enormous responsibility of the living church.

There is no way that we are going to be able to carry out this colossal responsibility in terms of the works of the kingdom without being supernaturally equipped to do so. This is where the spiritual gifts come in. Even Jesus himself was supernaturally equipped to do his works by the Holy Spirit. He did not do the things that he did by virtue of who he intrinsically was, God in the flesh, but in dependence on the Father, in the Holy Spirit, in the same way as God originally intended for man. This is obvious from many things he said about himself or that the gospel writers say about him. In John 14.10 he says, 'The Father who dwells in me does his works' and in Luke 5.17 we read, 'And the power of the Lord was with him to heal'. In Jesus, God became a real human like us, so that the day would come when we could do the same works that he did, equipped by the same Holy Spirit. As he put it in John 14.12, 'Truly, truly, I say to you, he who believes in me will also do the works that I do; and greater works than these will he do, because I go to the Father.' And he later expresses it in John 16.7, 'If I do not go away, the Counsellor will not come to you; but if I go, I will send him to you.' The Holy Spirit was poured out at Pentecost in order that the people of God might do the works of the kingdom.

There are clearly a number of quite specific motivating gifts that God gives to different members of the body. Paul lists some examples in Romans 12.4–8. Those that relate to the works of the kingdom are particularly the gifts of serving, contributing or sharing, and doing acts of mercy. This means that we can expect that among the community of God's people there will be those who, if given room, will develop these gifts in such a way as to motivate the body in the works of the kingdom. It may be to serve the practical needs of those who need help, as with the example of the deacons who were chosen to administer the daily distribution to the widows and fatherless in such a way as would overcome the charges of racism and prejudice. Or it may be to generate sharing in terms of families, belongings, homes, money or land. The word translated 'share' here, literally means 'to give a part'. It is the word used by John the Baptist when he described practical repentance in Luke 3.11: 'He who has two coats, let him share with him who has none; and he who has food, let him do likewise.'

It will be in the area of identifying and finding ways of meeting the crying needs of those who need mercy and compassion; the bereaved, the sick, the demonised, the prisoners and the neglected and powerless generally.

Then there are the obviously supernatural gifts of the Spirit which help us to engage in these ministries in ways which will really break through against the enemy and see God's kingdom established strongly. Paul lists some of these in 1 Corinthians 12.4–11. These are particularly the word of wisdom, the word of knowledge, faith, gifts of healing, the working of miracles, prophecy, the ability to discern spirits, tongues and the interpretation of tongues. All these have an important part to play if we are to work for the kingdom in the power of the Holy Spirit. They are simply aspects of the Spirit's work as we see them in Jesus' ministry. Jesus had many words of wisdom, especially when encountering difficult or dangerous questions from the Pharisees. In Luke 21.15 he promises the same to his followers: 'And I will give you a mouth and wisdom, which none of your adversaries will be able to contradict.' The Greek for 'mouth' here particularly signifies 'a word of mouth'. An example of a word of special knowledge or perception would be when Jesus told the woman at the well to fetch her husband and that she was five times married and currently living with someone she was not married to. It had such power in her life that she later said in John 4.39, ‘Come, see a man that told me all that I ever did. Can this be the Christ?’ Similarly it was a gift of faith that Jesus exercised when he spoke to the fig tree and it withered instantly. He was using gifts of healing virtually continually, worked miracles over wine and bread and fish, prophesied the destruction of the temple, discerned dumb and deaf spirits and so on. None of these supernatural activities were for the sake of it, but all led on to breakthroughs in the works of the kingdom, for healing and deliverance and the blessing of the poor. The only gifts of the Spirit not overtly described as a fundamental part of Jesus’ ministry are tongues and the interpretation of tongues. To me it is obvious that he spoke in tongues, because of the great outflow of tongues that followed his pouring out of the Spirit at Pentecost and because of their importance in my own life in the release of the Holy Spirit to accomplish the works of the kingdom. I speak in tongues quite a lot of the time and wish that everyone did, like Paul. Whatever, this one thing is for sure, Jesus put the highest possible priority on intimacy with his Father in the Spirit. An intimacy particularly expressed by the ecstatic little love word ‘abba’, and his delight in hearing the praise that came from the mouths of babes and sucklings. As he put it in Matthew 11.25–26, ‘You have hidden these things from the wise and understanding and revealed them to babes; yes, Father, for such was your gracious will.’ It would be surprising if at least this much ecstasy was not part of the promise of the Father which Jesus poured out upon his followers in this final stage of the coming in of his kingdom from Pentecost onwards.

(iii) The works of the kingdom in practice

(a) Liberating the poor

Jesus came to show us the kingdom of God, died and rose to overcome all the obstacles to it, and poured out his Spirit so that his church might receive and bear all the fruits of it, receive the gifts of it and do the work of it. The tragedy has been that so few have really got on with it. Some have attempted the work without the Spirit, others have embraced the Spirit without the work. Still others have seen the power of the cross to forgive but not its implications for receiving the kingdom of God. If we can only get our act together in the Holy Ghost in our generation then we will yet see the final great push for the kingdom of God in our time. This is what God wants. We must not let him down again.

In what has come to be called the Nazareth Manifesto in Luke 4.18–19, Jesus puts the poor first. So shall we. 'The Spirit of the Lord is upon me, because he has anointed me to preach good news to the poor.' The word poor here literally means 'one who crouches and cowers, a beggar'. Jesus is referring to the physically poor. These are the same ones that Jesus reassures John are having the good news preached to them as the proof of his Messiahship. These are the poor that the kingdom belongs to in Luke 6.20: 'Blessed are you poor, for yours is the kingdom of God.'

To preach good news to the poor is to tell them that the kingdom of God belongs to them. To do the works of the gospel for the poor is to give it to them, if they will receive it. The kingdom of God, as we saw in chapter one, restores our relationship with God as Father. It gives us our true value and honour. This is very fundamental, and many of us who have been poor found it difficult to receive God in this way. Poverty does not only rob a person of food, clothes, and housing, but it steals their worth and value, tells them lies about themselves and God, and so damages and dishonours their spirit. This is why the devil loves it so much. Sometimes poverty is the result of family breakdown, sickness or death. These experiences can similarly speak into a person's spirit that they are worthless and that God does not really care, or is unable to help them. Poverty is always the result of a broken society, into which the demons have found access. Where a society is just and gives room for God's kingdom there will be no poverty. This was God's promise to Israel in Deuteronomy 15.4: 'But there will be no poor among you, for the Lord will bless you in the land . . .' The poor are frequently oppressed by demons as well as lied to and damaged in spirit. Not all poor people are poor in spirit, but most are. All this explains why the Lord is biased to the poor, and why the church must be too. It is to redress the rejection they have received and been wounded by. This is why Isaiah includes 'healing the broken hearted' after 'preaching good news for the poor' in his original prophecy of the Lord Jesus in Isaiah 61. So giving the kingdom to the poor always requires close identification with them by the people of God, valuing and honouring them just as Jesus honoured the outcast lady at the well in John 4, and wanted to receive from her as well as give to her. The Father's love, and the relationship he desires is revealed in our love and the relationship we offer. Jesus never patronised the poor or showed them partiality. He treated them altogether as his equals in the sight of God, responsible for their actions. He told both the penniless paralytic and the woman taken in adultery to 'sin no more'. This is the great difference between bias and partiality. Bias chooses the penniless long-term cripple as the target of compassion, and honours him as a person with his own measure of responsibility for his situation and spiritual condition. Proverbs tells us not to show partiality to the poor in a law suit, that only robs him of his true worth as equally as his poverty has done. In the context of love and honour the Holy Spirit will show the difference between the damage done by others, and the personal sin that has kept God away. Then the good news will make sense and the person will be able to receive the Lord if they will. Then the healing process really begins.

In the kingdom of God we are also put right with our fellow men and women. The gospel of the kingdom reinstates the poor. In the kingdom all have equal value, standing and opportunity. One of the ways we serve the poor is by working to make this a reality. The church is the visual aid of the gospel. To build a church which is a genuine expression of the kingdom serves the poor. For there the kingdom is truly available to them. In the community of Jesus they will no longer be poor. They will be a valuable member of the house of God, a saint, a fellow heir with Jesus. This is no theoretical stuff. It has to be true. James is very strong about this in James 2.1–6:

> 'My brethren, show no partiality as you hold the faith of our Lord Jesus Christ, the Lord of glory. For if a man with gold rings and in fine clothing comes into your assembly, and a poor man in shabby clothing also comes in, and you pay attention to the one who wears the fine clothing and say, "Have a seat here, please", while you say to the poor man, "Stand there", or, "Sit at my feet", have you not made distinction among yourselves, and become judges with evil thoughts? Listen, my beloved brethren. Has not God chosen those who are poor in the world to be rich in faith and heirs to the kingdom which he has promised to those who love him?'

There is to be no classism in the church, just as there is to be no racism or sexism. Once again we must avoid partiality in all its forms. We may be biased, seeking to give room and help to those who are poor or to minority groups, but never must we insult or further dishonour people by falling in to tokenism instead of recognising gift in terms of spiritual function and growth. The fundamental entrance qualification to the kingdom is new birth, and for the work of the kingdom the fulness of the Spirit. These are the paramount riches which we seek to provide.

Nevertheless the church is a place of redistribution in real terms. There must be no poverty among us. This is where the gifts of contribution, of sharing come in. They need developing and mobilising through housegroups or other patterns of pastoral care and common life. The early church experience of Acts 4.32–35 is normative and we must find similar appropriate ways of expressing it today.

> 'Now the company of those who believed were of one heart and soul, and no one said that any of the things which he possessed was his own, but they had everything in common. And with great power the apostles gave their testimony to the resurrection of the Lord Jesus, and great grace was upon them all. There was not a needy person among them, for as many as were possessors of lands or houses sold them, and brought the proceeds of what was sold and laid it at the apostles' feet; and distribution was made to each as any had need.'

Not only is the production of a living community for the poor one of the works of the kingdom, but it is part of our evangelism to so salt society that the roots of poverty can be exposed and dealt with. We have to be seen to be doing this if our gospel to the poor is to have any credibility. We must work for justice against the demonic powers of materialism, power and position where they are breaking through the government and social administration of the day and producing or affirming poverty. This whole area of the work of the kingdom is so fundamental that we will be spending a good deal of the final chapter looking at it.

Finally, the good news of the kingdom is that we can be put right with the whole created order. This strikes at the very heart of poverty. Poverty is totally against God's will for us. God's purpose for Israel in Jeremiah 29.11 is his purpose for all mankind in the kingdom of God. 'I know the plans I have for you, says the Lord, plans for welfare and not for evil, to give you a future and a hope.'

The works of the kingdom must demonstrate this to the poor. The works of healing and deliverance play their part in this, as we shall consider shortly. But practical acts of mercy and sharing with the poor are utterly essential to evangelism. In 1975 a group of us began to work among young people on the streets of Sydenham, in the London borough of Lewisham. We invited local youngsters to help us as local Christians to discover the spiritual and material needs of our neighbourhood. They discovered lots of material need, especially among elderly folk. There was great need of companionship, practical help with odd jobs about the house, garden or flat, and emergency support in times of sickness or frailty, particularly where the social services were unable or insufficiently sensitive to cope. In the process of the project a good bunch of youngsters came to the Lord. They were unanimous about the way ahead for them as far as evangelism was concerned. We must offer practical help for the needy as far as we feasibly could. This was part of kingdom evangelism in their eyes, and they were right.

Our whole Jesus Action work of neighbour love began. Through the years it has been a fundamental part of the integrity of the witness that the Holy Spirit has helped us to give. For anyone in doubt about the need for this kind of evangelism in London, within days of placing an article about our offer of help in a local free newspaper we were beginning to be inundated with calls from desperately overloaded social workers, and I was asked to discuss our work with the local senior social worker. These days Ichthus has grown so much that our contacts come equally from our own encounters with the poor in our evangelism generally.

(b) Healing the sick

Jesus did an enormous amount of healing, as did his disciples, who like us were commissioned to continue his work. It is remarkable that the healing works of the gospel have ever been regarded as a matter of question. Approximately half the chapters of the synoptic gospels contain direct references to Jesus' healing ministry. Many of the descriptions they give are very far reaching. This is also true of the numerous references to healings in the Acts of the Apostles. Matthew describes the terrific scope of Jesus' activities in healing in Matthew 4.23–25 and 9.35:

> 'And he went about all Galilee, teaching in their synagogues and preaching the gospel of the kingdom and healing every disease and every infirmity among the people. So his fame spread throughout all Syria, and they brought him all the sick, those afflicted with various diseases and pains, demoniacs, epileptics, and paralytics, and he healed them . . . And Jesus went about all the cities and villages, teaching in their synagogues and preaching the gospel of the kingdom, and healing every disease and every infirmity.'

Luke continues our overall picture with particular reference to the disciples in Luke 9.1–2, 6 and Luke 10.1–2, 8–9:

> 'And he called the twelve together and gave them power and authority over all demons and to cure diseases, and he sent them out to preach the kingdom and to heal . . . And they departed and went through the villages, preaching the gospel and healing everywhere . . . After this the Lord appointed seventy others . . . And he said to them . . . "whenever you enter a town and they receive you, eat what is set before you; heal the sick in it and say to them, 'The kingdom of God has come near you'." '

Luke completes the overview with his accounts of some of Peter and Paul's experiences in Acts 5.12, 14–16 and 19.11:

> 'Now many signs and wonders were done among the people by the apostles . . . And more than ever believers were added to the Lord, multitudes both of men and women, so that they even carried out the sick into the streets, and laid them on beds and pallets, that as Peter came by at least his shadow might fall on some of them. The people also gathered from the towns around Jerusalem, bringing the sick and those afflicted with unclean spirits and they were all healed . . . And God did extraordinary miracles by the hands of Paul, so that handkerchiefs or aprons were carried away from his body to the sick, and diseases left them and the evil spirits came out of them.'

Several factors stand out immediately from these accounts, the enormous success of Jesus and his disciples in healing, its widespread impact, and the numerical increase in Jesus' followers which resulted. Where this work of supernatural healing is occurring today, although success is generally less universal and the impact consequently less widespread, the numerical growth of the church is nonetheless increasing. We must press on to greater breakthrough in this part of evangelism if we are to give adequate expression to the quality and power of God's compassion, and experience the level of numerical growth required to get the good news into all the world in our generation.

A number of things are required of us if we are going to achieve this. We must preach the same good news as Jesus did, and follow it through to its logical conclusion. That is to say we must declare him as able and willing to heal the physical, psychological and spiritual sickness of men and women. Then we must follow his example in simple obedient faith. We must place our hands on the sick and pray for them to be healed. We must anoint them with oil, touch them, rebuke the demons in them, tell them to go wash in a local pool and all the other kinds of things that Jesus did in response to the prompting of the Spirit. We must determine to learn to hear what the Holy Spirit is saying in each situation. At the same time we must discover and attack vigorously those wrong attitudes and demonic powers which even restricted Jesus' healing work at times and are therefore likely to be current restrictions on the power of Jesus to heal today. One thing is unavoidable, we are going to have to stick our necks out, risk failure, embarrassment and misunderstanding. This is what many of us have been doing lately, with no small success, for which we praise God. There is much yet to be done, but enough is happening to make it quite clear that the good news of the kingdom is still the news of Jesus' power and willingness to heal the sick. As Matthew reminds us in chapter 8.17, 'This was to fulfil what was spoken by the prophet Isaiah, "He took our infirmities and bore our diseases".'

God has not changed, this has always been part of his purpose for mankind, ever since sin entered the world and with it the onslaught of death and sickness. When he first established his covenant with the Jews in Exodus 15. 25–26 this was part of the whole intention.

> 'The Lord made for them a statute and an ordinance and there he proved them, saying, "If you will diligently hearken to the voice of the Lord your God, and do that which is right in his eyes, and give heed to his commandments and keep all his statutes, I will put none of these diseases upon you which I put on the Egyptians; for I am the Lord, your healer".'

Our experience so far has been that the best opportunities of praying for the sick arise after presenting healing as part of the good news while visiting from house to house, or at the end of a large meeting when those who wish for prayer for healing are encouraged to come forward. Other opportunities arise by request from those who hear of healings happening or who respond to James 4.14–15:

> 'Is any among you sick? let him call for the elders of the church, and let them pray over him, anointing him with oil in the name of the Lord; and the prayer of faith will save the sick man, and the Lord will raise him up.'

But in these cases too, prayer in the context of worship and corporate faith in a large meeting seems to get the best results. The reason for this, I'm sure, is the huge backlog of unbelief and spiritual damage which is the sad heritage of much of contemporary western Christianity. Only very Spirit-filled environments seem to be able to shift this at all easily. Wonderfully, the kingdom of God is again drawing near in our generation to change all this. Healing is a sign of this kingdom. When the kingdom of heaven comes for ever there will be no more sickness, pain, death or tears. Revelation 21.1–4 makes this very clear.

> 'Then I saw a new heaven and a new earth; for the first heaven and the first earth had passed away, and the sea was no more. And I saw the holy city, new Jerusalem, coming down out of heaven from God, prepared as a bride adorned for her husband; and I heard a loud voice from the throne saying, "Behold, the dwelling of God is with men. He will dwell with them, and they shall be his people, and God himself will be with them; he will wipe away every tear from their eyes, and death shall be no more, neither shall there be mourning nor crying nor pain any more, for the former things have passed away".'

Our good news is that this kingdom is breaking into the present through the life and work of the Lord Jesus and his outpoured Spirit. We are those, as Paul describes in 1 Corinthians 10.11,'upon whom the end of the ages has come', or as the writer to the Hebrews puts it in chapter 6.5,'who have tasted . . . the powers of the age to come.' Healing is the evidence of this. We must declare and reach out for more and more of this kingdom. When it is preached in all the earth Jesus will return at last and sickness and death will be overcome for ever. Until then we love, preach and fight on in the Holy Spirit. Some battles we lose. Just as some people don't get converted, some don't get healed. We don't necessarily blame either. There are several possible reasons why a person doesn't get converted. It may be my fault, their fault, society's fault, the church's fault, certainly Satan's fault. But it is never God's will that a person doesn't receive his kingdom. This applies to the whole of salvation, including healing. Because of the variety of possible reasons why a person is sick we need supernatural wisdom to know how best to minister healing to them. Apart from the gifts of healing themselves three essentials here are the word of knowledge, the word of wisdom and the discernment of spirits. The word of knowledge can show us the root of the problem and the word of wisdom can tell us when and how to use the insight. The discernment of spirits applies to discerning the activity of evil spirits in causing sickness, and also to discerning the state of a person's own spirit, which information can be crucial in understanding why a person is sick or whether or not they are ready or willing to receive help. If God shows us the root of a problem then we are half way to solving it. We can pray in faith when we sense that God has given special insight into the problem. Often then we can actually see the healing taking place in the Spirit. Then we ask and receive. Jesus said in John 5.19, 'Truly, truly, I say to you, the Son can do nothing of his own accord, but only what he sees the Father doing; for whatever he does, that the Son does likewise.' We had exactly that experience several weeks ago when praying for a man with a growth on his thyroid. While praying I had a distinct picture of the growth being taken by a hand and removed. When we had finished praying it had completely disappeared.

We need to develop these spiritual gifts if we are to be effective in the work of the kingdom. Fortunately they are catching! Our experience has been that if you get alongside spiritual men and women who are using these gifts then you can begin to move into them too. I first really began to move ahead in the realm of receiving words of knowledge in the form of spiritual pictures in this way. The same has been true in the realm of gifts of healing. I've never forgotten the experience of watching people's damaged legs growing as I sat alongside Ian Andrews when a group of us got together with him for a conference on the use of spiritual gifts in healing. But even more faith building was the experience of then reaching out my own hand and feeling the extraordinary shift within a damaged knee as I asked the Lord to replace the damaged cartilage and he did!

(c) Casting out demons

As we saw in chapter three, the breakthrough of Satan into families, governments and churches releases hosts of demons into the world which prey upon the lives of men and women. Paul faces this fairly and squarely when he writes in Ephesians 6.12:

> 'For we are not contending against flesh and blood, but against the principalities, against the powers, against the world rulers of this present darkness, against the spiritual hosts of wickedness in the heavenly places.'

Jesus came to destroy all this, and it is a crucial part of the work of his kingdom to get the devil off people's backs. Getting started on this is not as difficult as it might seem. As we move further on into a genuinely kingdom experience, obeying Jesus, enjoying the intensity of his presence as we fellowship together in the Holy Spirit, engaging in spiritual warfare, declaring his words, doing his works and denouncing the powers of evil, then the demons will manifest themselves just as they did with Jesus at the beginning. Then we must cast them out as he commanded us to. This is unavoidably the work of the kingdom. This was an integral part of what the apostles were commissioned for in Mark 3.14–15: 'And he appointed twelve, to be with him, and to be sent out to preach and have authority to cast out demons.' We can have real confidence in this authority which Jesus gives us. It is right to remember the warning of Jesus to his disciples that they rejoice in their relationship with him and not their power over demons. But he still reminded them in Luke 10.19, 'I have given you authority over all the power of the enemy; and nothing shall hurt you.'

It is important to understand that this authority is in the name of Jesus and specifically evidenced in his blood. The disciples rejoiced because 'even the demons are subject to us *in your name*' and in Revelation 12.11 the saints are described as overcoming Satan 'by *the blood* of the Lamb'.

Jesus overcame Satan in his life as he repeatedly chose the kingdom way of love, and in his death his poured out blood was the final revelation of that love in the face of the worst that Satan's anti-kingdom could do to God or man. As John put it in John 13.1, 'Jesus . . . having loved his own who were in the world, loved them to the end.' It was just that 'end' point that proved the supremacy of life over death, of love over hate, of forgiveness over sin and of Jesus over Satan. To call on the name of the Lord and speak of the blood he shed is to assert that victorious end point of the kingdom of heaven over the power of hell. The key is to cast the demons out in the context of strong love for the person, humble faith in the name and the blood of Jesus and with verbal aggression towards the demons. Then they have to yield.

Although the casting out of demons is an unpleasant business, it brings great joy afterwards. This is because it is not only a sign of the kingdom but actually brings the kingdom in. The spiritual air is cleared, another dwelling for God is opened up in the human race and the fulfilment of the eternal purpose of God brought another step nearer. This is wonderful! As Jesus put it in Matthew 12.28, 'If it is by the Spirit of God that I cast out demons, then the kingdom of God has come upon you.'

One rather alarming discovery that comes to light as soon as the intensity of the Holy Spirit's presence grows among the people of God is that Christians have demonic problems as well as non-Christians. On reflection, I suppose it must have been a rather similar shock when the demons first started manifesting themselves among the worshippers in the synagogues at the beginning of Jesus' ministry. This has given some people, including me, a few theological problems, although it's been necessary to put off answering them until after dealing with the demons! However, once we understand and accept the war-strategy of Satan in breaking the cover of family, government and church and penetrating them with his powerful antivalues, then we begin to see how Christians as well as non-Christians can be affected this way. Some people have suggested a difference between demon oppression and demon possession, others a difference between impersonal Satanic forces and personal demonic presences which they precede or follow. These distinctions make a lot of sense and certainly suggest a variety of degrees of demonic influence. Whereas it is hard to envisage how a Christian could be completely possessed by demons, it is not difficult to see how they become oppressed and affected in lesser but still very real and damaging ways. However, when it comes down to the practical remedy it doesn't make much difference. The demonic influence still needs casting out.

Satan gets his hooks into people in two ways. Firstly, he does it by deceiving them into giving a bit of themselves away to him in return for some special knowledge or pleasure. This is what happens when people get involved in the occult through horoscopes, ouija boards, fortune tellers and the like. Secondly, he attaches himself to people because demons delight in infesting the spiritual hurts and wounds caused by dehumanising experiences, rather as flies swarm around physical wounds. The devil's first ever deceit against the human race at the fall, gave him a foothold which he continues to use. There he lied to Eve about the physical, mental, and spiritual satisfaction she would achieve in turn for submitting her will to him. This is still his tactic. The tragic downfall of Judas Iscariot illuminates the way in which Satan gradually increases his grip on a person's life. He had been appointed with the rest of the twelve to be with Jesus, to preach the gospel of the kingdom and to have authority over Satan. Instead he gave way to Satanic pressure through lust for money. John tells us in John 12.6, 'he was a thief, and as he had the money bag he used to take what was put into it'. At this point there is no suggestion that he was demonised, simply that he habitually gave way to the influence of the Satanic kingdom. Subsequently Satan's influence in his life is described more strongly, as he considered betraying Jesus, in John 13.2:'When the devil had already put it into the heart of Judas Iscariot, Simon's son, to betray him . . .' Now the habitual lust for things amounted to giving away part of his heart to Satan and allowing something really demonic to lodge there. Finally, in John 13.27, 'Satan entered into him.' This is the process whereby sin gives way to Satan more and more until oppression and even possession can take place.

The whole realm of the occult is the product of Satan's strategy to offer satisfaction to our physical needs and give us power and status over our fellow men and women in return for a foothold into our wills and spirits. Even when a person becomes a Christian he can't easily give to the Lord what is already clearly given away to Satan, and this may explain the phenomenon of the professing Christian who is still clearly troubled by demonic powers. Once Satan gains this kind of foothold he seeks to gain further ground, either by the same process or by playing into the hurts and wounds that come our way in life as a result of moving out of the cover of God's grace and into the darkness. When the God-given responsibility of government is subverted by the powers of Satan to promote the lust for possessions, power and position at the expense of people, as has so often happened in the history of mankind and is happening right now, then the human spirit is exposed to the hurts and wounds of poverty, worthlessness, rejection, racism, sexism, classism and so on, whether or not people have themselves consciously opened up to direct contact with the demonic. The demons then aim for these hurts and are particularly able to attach themselves to them where the individual's response to them is a sinful one. Fear, bitterness, jealousy, resentment and self-pity are the breeding grounds for demonic activity, however understandable such wrong reactions might be.

It was exactly this dreadful complex of Satanic breakthrough that ultimately produced the Canaanites, about whom God said in Deuteronomy 18.9–12:

> 'When you come into the land which the Lord your God gives you, you shall not learn to follow the abominable practices of those nations. There shall not be found among you any one who makes his son or his daughter pass through fire, any one who practises divination, a soothsayer, or an augur, or a sorcerer, or

> a charmer, or a medium, or a wizard, or a necromancer. For whoever does these things is an abomination to the Lord; and because of these abominable practices the Lord your God is driving them out before you.'

Many, perhaps most, people today have been involved with these demonic practices and are badly damaged both by them and the spiritual hurts that preceded or followed them. People like this become the prey of Satan and the embodiment of his kingdom. This is the last thing God wants, and Jesus and his kingdom are here to destroy all the works of the devil in their lives. No longer is it necessary to physically wipe out such a people in order to overcome Satan's kingdom and preserve the kingdom of God. Jesus has stood in their place and loved them to the end. His name and his blood can set them free if they are willing. The church of Jesus is here to overcome the works of Satan. We must get on with it.

But this is not the end of the story. Tragically the church has not only frequently failed to destroy the works of Satan but has instead given way to them. Instead of becoming the protective environment for the kingdom of God it has become itself a place of demonic activity. This is the primary reason why Christians find themselves oppressed by demonic problems. James explains this succinctly in James 3.14–16:

> 'But if you have bitter jealousy and selfish ambition in your hearts, do not boast and be false to the truth. This wisdom is not such as comes down from above, but is earthly, unspiritual, devilish. For where jealousy and selfish ambition exist, there will be disorder and every vile practice.'

Many Christian leaders over the years have allowed the church itself to become a place where hurts and wounds of spirit are received instead of healed. Even occult practices have been given a place; dead people are prayed to and occult objects worshipped. As a result evil religious spirits prey on people's lives. Several years ago my wife Sue and I were praying with a girl who had occult involvement. As sometimes happens the Lord gave me a spiritual picture. Usually these are to give insight to help the person. This time it was of an occult divining pendulum. Then I realised that it was something back in my own life that the Holy Spirit was reminding me about. I was about ten years of age. A well known Bible teacher of those days was visiting our church. He was being entertained by my parents. At the meal table he asked whether the food had been prepared in an aluminium container. He was of the opinion that aluminium caused cancer. My mother was unsure what her pots and pans were made of. At which point this Bible teacher produced an ivory divining pendulum and hung it over the meal. It worked very well. So he encouraged us all to have a go. I had to repent of that involvement then and there as the Lord reminded me of it. Such vile practices seriously threaten the kingdom of God. But they only creep in when the Satanic powers of covetousness and personal ambition break through among the people of God. Jesus warned his contemporaries in Matthew 12.43–45:

> 'When the unclean spirit has gone out of a man, he passes through the waterless places seeking rest, but he finds none. Then he says, "I will return to my house from which I came." And when he comes he finds it empty, swept and put in order. Then he goes and brings with him seven other spirits more evil than himself, and they enter and dwell there; and the

last state of that man becomes worse than the first. So shall it be with this evil generation.'

May God help us today to so love one another and get on with the business of chasing the devil out of the lives of men and women that this won't happen to our generation.

Even as I have been writing this evening a lady came to see me who had long term involvement with an occult healer both before and since her conversion to Christ. Earlier I had been aware that an enemy stream of influence somehow played into her life. Now she is free from it. Firstly I asked the Father to bind the power of Satan in the name of Jesus. Then she confessed to the Lord and repudiated her involvement in the devil's deception. After that I told Satan and his demons to clear out in Jesus' name and by his blood and take all their lying influence away to the place Jesus has prepared for them. Then she told Satan to push off too. Finally we prayed for the Holy Spirit to flood those areas which had previously been under the influence of the enemy in her spirit, soul and body.

Sometimes the Lord indicates the particular type of Satanic influence or actual demon that is present. Then it is possible to name it specifically and cast it out with even greater confidence. As far as I can work it out demons take on various characters and forms of behaviour in keeping with the three main areas of Satanic power which Jesus encountered in the temptations as we saw in chapter three. The lust for bread and physical fulfilment would include demons of greed, lust and addiction and so on; the lust for power over others involve demons of violence, anger, murder and racism; and the lust for status and position include spirits of pride, jealousy, ambition and self pity. Probably all the works of the flesh in Galatians 5.19–21 can become the manifestations of actual demons if they are given way to for long enough, just as Satan entered Judas on the back of his greed for money. Whatever, we should be as specific as the Holy Spirit helps us to be and then go for it! Perhaps it hardly needs saying that as far as possible we should always operate together with others in the fellowship of the Holy Spirit as we go about this, as with the other works of the kingdom.

Chapter 6

Kingdom Warnings

We have already seen that in both word and deed Jesus denounced, warned and proclaimed judgement and woe to the establishment leaders of his day, where their actions were destructive of the kingdom of God. We saw that although this may not sound like good news, for the poor and for all who long for the kingdom of God, it is very good news indeed. This is an important and too often neglected part of evangelism. It is not hard to understand why this is so. For a start it has clear political implications and it is easy to end up simply playing into the hands of the right, left or centre, in terms of one political power structure or another. Some Christians seem to have done this and a lot of us don't want to fall into the same trap. But if we have the Holy Spirit to guide us, there is no need for this to happen. He carries the life of Jesus and his kingdom. After all Jesus knew what he was doing and so can we. The real crunch is that it is going to cost a lot, the more we obey Jesus on this one. This was what got him crucified and we know it. If we follow through on this we may begin to discover why we haven't had too much persecution in the West lately. Some of us are going to be in gaol some of the time. That is not to be sought after, but it is a real possibility. Some might get killed, like Jesus was. As he put it in Matthew 10.17:

> 'Beware of men; for they will deliver you up to councils, and flog you in their synagogues, and you will be dragged before governors and kings for my sake, to bear testimony before them and the Gentiles . . . A disciple is not above his teacher, nor a servant above his master . . . have no fear of them; for nothing is covered that will not be revealed, or hidden that will not be known. What I tell you in the dark, utter in the light; and what you hear whispered, proclaim upon the housetops.'

There are several major breakthroughs in understanding this aspect of kingdom evangelism which we need to look at. These have to do with the relationship of the kingdom of God to the kingdoms of this world, the existence of universal justice norms for the nations, and the meaning of Peter and Paul's teaching on Christian subjection to government institutions.

(i) The kingdom of God and kingdoms of this world

Christians are not agreed about the relationship of the kingdom of God to the kingdoms of this world. Many still take the view that the work of the kingdom of God is to take over the structures and institutions of this world. Then there will be Christian art, hospitals, schools, judiciary, unions, businesses, co-operatives and ultimately a Christian government and a Christian society. The proponents of this view may differ as to whether it would constitute the final coming in of the kingdom or whether Jesus will return at some point and finish the job off. But they agree on the direction and strategy which the work of the kingdom should take. According to them, the kingdom will come through the invasion of the existing structures of society by

Christians, maybe changing or inventing a few structures along the way. In essence this is the process begun long ago when the Roman emperor Constantine first had his vision of the sign of the cross in which he believed he would conquer. Of course many Christians who take this view disagree with the way Constantine and thousands after him went about it. But the fundamental vision remains the same.

Other Christians take a quite different view. They regard the kingdom of God as altogether different from the kingdom of this world. This world has had it, they say, and is only going to get worse. For them the kingdom of God is seen either as an individual personal relationship with God or as the believing church. In this model the kingdom is rather like a greenhouse for getting ready for heaven, or a lifeboat for getting there in. Relationships with the kingdoms of this world vary from virtual retreat into monasticism, to outreach into the world as a fishing ground for more fish for the boat, or a seed bed for more plants for the greenhouse. At its worst this view allows for some Christians to feel that they are safe from responsibility to the world while at the same time making a pretty comfortable living in it while they wait to be taken off into heaven when the world collapses into hell.

Neither of these opinions of the kingdom was the one Jesus held. He came proclaiming the kingdom of God in the context of the struggle and debate between two or even three already existing kingdoms competing for power over God's people Israel, who, as we have seen, really symbolised God's whole world. For it was to be through them that all the nations of the earth were to be blessed. But now they were overrun, occupied by a peculiarly uneasy partnership of conflicting kingdoms. The spiritually subverted rule of Herod and the Sanhedrin, and the politically imperialistic power of Rome. Into this volatile confusion came Jesus, proclaiming another kingdom altogether. The rightful and true kingdom of God that Israel and the whole earth was made for. The kingdom he proclaimed challenged the kingdoms of this world to their very roots. He called Herod a fox, the rulers of the Jews children of Satan and informed Pilate that the imperialistic power of Rome was only by the temporary permission of his Father. Yet he disdained Herod's palace, proclaimed the total destruction of the whole Jewish temple and establishment and refused to let Pilate help him. Nor would he allow the mass of common folk to make him their king by force.

In absolute terms, the structures of the kingdoms of this world are entirely irrelevant to the kingdom of God. When it comes in its consummation there will be no hospitals for no one will be sick, there will be no schools because we won't need anyone to teach us, there will be no multinational corporations because everyone will have their own vine and fig tree equivalent, and there will be no judiciary because there will be no criminals, and the throne of God and of the Lamb will be its government. On the other hand, the structures of this world's kingdoms do have a limited and necessary function which Jesus acknowledged. This function is to preserve the nations from going over the top in rebellion and sin to the degree that they usher in hell and lose the kingdom of God. As Paul put it in Athens in Acts 17.26-27:

> 'And he made from one every nation of men to live on all the face of the earth, having determined allotted periods and the boundaries of their habitation, that they should seek God, in the hope that they might feel after him and find him.'

Jesus said his followers have a responsibility to help the leaders of those nations to do that. To be salt and light to them. Some need to become lawyers, politicians, educationalists, union members and so on, like Joseph and Daniel did. We need to speak out and demonstrate and help the governing authorities to do their job properly. But as far as the coming in of the kingdom of God is concerned, that lies elsewhere, with the church, in the Holy Spirit, as we have already seen in the earlier chapters. At the heart of the kingdom of God, as far as this world is concerned, lies the church, who have been entrusted with the kingdom in the Holy Spirit. A new society, a radical alternative, an outpost of heaven, an upside down kingdom of love and justice. It must stay that way, serving the world with its good news of new life with the Father, new relationships with each other, and with the coming transformation of the whole created order already beginning in its wake. Once the good news of this kingdom gets into all the earth then Jesus will come and the institutions and authorities of this world will be replaced by his alternative loving throne everywhere. But if we don't understand the important role that the government institutions of the kingdoms of this world have in the process we will never get there. They must at least maintain the limits which God has set them. Otherwise the powers of hell will break all bounds and destroy the image of God in human lives and personalities. Then the Holy Spirit will be grieved away, the work of the kingdom thwarted and another generation will have lost its chance of bringing in the kingdom of God. This is on the brink of happening all over the world.

In order to help the established authorities to maintain at least the limits of justice, we need to understand more clearly from God's viewpoint what these boundaries are.

(ii) Justice norms for the nations

In chapter three we investigated the Satanic powers that pressurise families, governments and churches in the attempt to establish the anti-God values of Satan among the nations. We understood that government appears to be the particular arena for Satan's involvement because of his original authority as a senior spiritual ruler of this world. We looked at the temptations and saw that in basic terms the Satanic powers can be described as materialism, power lust and selfish ambition. I have suggested that the proper sphere of the established authorities of the kingdoms of this world is to limit the powers of sin and evil in the nations. Satan and his principalities and powers are of course working very hard against those limits.

The prophet Amos gives us very important insight into the nature of those limits and the way they relate to the pressure from the demonic powers. In the first two chapters of his prophecy, Amos makes clear that there are limits to the amount of materialism, power lust and selfish ambition which God is prepared to endure in the earth before taking away his hand and allowing judgement to fall. Amos clearly describes these limits in relation to six nations in the seventh century B.C. The first two nations, Syria and Philistia, had given way to materialism to such an extent that they treated people just like things. They were prepared to use military overkill in times of war, destroy innocent youths, children and pregnant women, and trade people for economic advantage. The second two nations, Tyre and Edom, had so given way to the lust for power and dominion over other nations that they were prepared to forget covenants of brotherhood and deliver up whole nations into oppression without mercy. The final two nations, Amnon and Moab, so gave way to pride and selfish ambition that they abused the weak and the needy, pregnant women, unborn children and prisoners of war. In each case the prophet's message was that they had gone right over the limits and now their established authorities would be broken and their nations exiled, destroyed, or overrun by their enemies. As each statement is given, Amos rings out the confirmation of God's final judgement: 'For three transgressions and for four, I will not revoke the punishment.'

Planned overkill in times of war, broken covenants of brotherhood, the destruction of unborn children, these are some of the limits God sets on the nations. These are the points where the limits of justice are broken and governments stand condemned by God. Such governments are without a future and their people uncovered, exposed to the unthinkable: exile, destruction and enemy occupation. But this is God's judgement on such nations. So the justice norms for the nations should be the *protection* of people from being treated like things, the *establishment* of brotherhood between nations and the *support* of the weak and the needy. In twentieth century western terms this at least means the abolition of nuclear weapons, the provision of aid to the third world and the protection of the unborn child.

The application of all this to western nations today, particularly Britain, is obvious. We have allowed nuclear weapons with the capacity for wild overkill in war to be set up on our soil, we have broken the moral agreement we made at UNCTAD 1972 to provide at lest 0.7% of our G.N.P. in overseas aid to the third world and in 1982 we aborted one in five of our unborn children. It is unequivocally the task of evangelism in Britain and similar nations to warn the government and its leaders of the situation they are in. We also need to warn the people generally. We need the Holy Spirit to show us how to do this, but we don't need the Holy Spirit to tell us it needs to be done. It is the obvious application of what he has already revealed in Jesus and the scriptures as a whole. At Ichthus so far we have written to all the members of the cabinet, shadow cabinet, local members of Parliament and the European Parliament on these issues, as well as the local councillors. We have published a pamphlet which we make widely available. We encourage the inter-church agencies like CARE and the Evangelical Alliance to address the problem also. We are needing the Holy Spirit to show us what to do next. But without doubt this is an important part of evangelism, and even if the government doesn't change its policies, the very existence of Christians speaking out clearly against these evils kicks the gates of hell and welcomes the Holy Spirit more into the British Isles. This is a move in the right direction. But we need some means to evaluate other aspects of government policy in the nations and localities God has placed us, to see whether the good news requires us to speak and act on other issues too. And we need guidelines for appropriate kingdom evangelism against these kinds of social evils.

(iii) Peter and Paul's teaching and behaviour towards government institutions

One common argument for not speaking or acting against government policy is Peter and Paul's teaching in 1 Peter 2.23–24 and Romans 13.1–4:

> 'Be subject for the Lord's sake to every human institution, whether it be to the emperor as supreme, or governors as sent by him to punish those who do wrong and to praise those who do right . . . let every

> person be subject to the governing authorities. For there is no authority except from God, and those that exist have been instituted by God. Therefore he who resists the authorities resists what God has appointed, and those who resist will incur judgement. For rulers are not a terror to good conduct but to bad. Would you have no fear of him who is in authority? Then do what is good, and you will receive his approval, for he is God's servant for your good.'

Now on the face of it this seems straightforward enough. Christians are to acquiesce to the authorities, or else they will be found to be resisting God and be judged. But this conclusion ignores two fundamental points. The first is that both Peter and Paul clearly state that the God given authority of governments is 'to punish those who do wrong and to praise those who do right' and 'a terror not to good conduct but to bad'. But this type of government is no problem to the work of the kingdom of God. The problem doesn't begin until governments are a terror to *good* conduct and are found to be praising what's *wrong* and terrorising what's *right*. The second point is that both Peter and Paul spoke right out and acted against government authorities that they found to be preventing good conduct and promoting the bad. This changes the whole picture. Both men who spoke the most conservatively about honouring authority, were also the most radical denouncers of those same authorities when they broke the bounds of justice and abused their position. In Acts 4.19, Peter said to the rulers and elders: '. . . Whether it is right in the sight of God to listen to you rather than to God, you must judge; for we cannot but speak of what we have seen and heard.'

Again in Acts 23.1–5 Paul spoke to the Council:

' "Brethren, I have lived before God in all good conscience up to this day." And the high priest Ananias commanded those who stood by him to strike him on the mouth. Then Paul said to him, "God shall strike you, you whitewashed wall! Are you sitting to judge me acording to the law, and yet contrary to the law you order me to be struck?" Those who stood by said, "Would you revile God's high priest?" And Paul said, "I did not know, brethren, that he was the high priest; for it is written, 'You shall not speak evil of a ruler of your people'." '

Both these incidents are as extraordinarily radical as the previous passages are conservative. Peter makes clear that authority has a limit beyond which Christians are not required to be subject, and Paul goes to the length of asserting a point beyond which authority is actually abdicated and to be spoken against. Some people have asserted that as these incidents both involve religious authorities the limits of government are only breached on religious issues. But this misses the whole point. The point is that they are breached, and when they are breached they may need to be spoken or acted against. Yet both 1 Peter 2 and Romans 13 appear to teach at surface level that this should never be done. Once we accept that it can be done, then it can be done on other issues apart from narrowly religious ones. In any case we have seen by this stage that evangelism is not only confined to 'religious' questions, but also matters of justice and good news for the poor. It remains for us to understand the real meaning of Peter and Paul's conservative statements, and to find any guidelines contained in them by which we can discover the limits and boundaries beyond which government must not go, and which constitute the grounds for the warnings of the gospel.

The unmistakeable message of 1 Peter 2 and Romans 13 is that God intends that there should be governing authorities, and that these authorities should be respected and upheld. Otherwise there can be no brakes or limits on sin and evil. This is a very important function, and so Christians must support it, and warn against those who are anarchistic and against authority. However, the equally unmistakeable message of Acts 4 and Acts 23 is that there are limits to the authority that governments have, and that Christians must speak out when governments break those limits. Peter, in particular, makes very clear what those limits are. For he tells us to be subject for the Lord's sake to every human institution, and then he continues in 1 Peter 2.16–17, 'Live as free men, yet without using your freedom as a pretext for evil; but live as servants of God. Honour all men. Love the brotherhood. Fear God. Honour the emperor.'

This is very illuminating. This is what Christians are to do while being 'subject'. What happens then, when the 'human institution' restricts freedom, promotes license, rejects a service model for living, dishonours people, prevents free association and denies freedom of worship? The answer is clear enough. In 1 Peter 2.15 he says, 'For it is God's will that by doing right you should put to silence the ignorance of foolish men.' In other words, these are our guidelines for civil disobedience. We must assert and follow them at all costs. Of course we shall need to be totally dependent on the Holy Spirit to know when and how to speak out or to act. And we shall be careful to uphold authority even as we denounce the failure of specific authorities. But do it we must. This is not an optional extra. This is all part of being faithful to the good news of the kingdom of our Lord Jesus.

These guidelines give us our agenda for this aspect of

evangelism today. The injunction to live as free men, but without using our freedom as a pretext for evil has many current applications. Most obviously, it has much to say about conservative economic policy in the western world. Freedom to grow rich and expand profits at the expense of the unemployed and the third world falls in this category. Whether or not the fruits of economic expansion may one day trickle down to the poor is not the point. The point is that at this moment one group's freedom is at another group's expense. This breaks the boundaries that God has set. We must speak out and act for a fair redistribution of wealth and power. On the other hand, the increasing concentration of power and influence in the hands of the state must equally be spoken and acted against. Full state control of education, industry, welfare or the media only robs people of their freedom and responsibility in the end. The job of government is to protect us from the evil powers and to give room for the kingdom of God, not to replace it. This kind of gospel gets us into trouble equally with all political parties!

The injunction to honour all people outlaws racism, sexism and classism. We cannot honour everyone while government institutions promote or allow such distinctions to put people down. Here again is our agenda for words and actions. The gospel of Jesus is implacably opposed to such forms of oppression. Similarly, when any government seeks to prevent free association and freedom of worship they are to be spoken against and disobeyed as the Lord shows the way. He cleansed the temple, turned over the money changers' tables, broke the law by healing on the Sabbath day, told popular stories at the expense of the instituted authorities and denounced them publicly. He is our example and our king.

In Romans 13.8, Paul gives us our solid base line: 'Owe

no one anything, except to love one another.'

This must be the motivation and the context of all we do. We may be misunderstood, but we must never move outside of the Holy Spirit in this. The works of the flesh, as we considered in chapter five, cannot ever be the works of the kingdom of God. Paul reminds Timothy in 2 Timothy 2. 24–26:

> 'The Lord's servant must not be quarrelsome, but kind to everyone, an apt teacher, forbearing, correcting his opponents with gentleness. God may perhaps grant that they will repent and come to know the truth, and they may escape from the snare of the devil, after being captured by him to do his will.'

In the name of Jesus, with love and humility, we insist that the governing authorities act as God intends. Not by human might or power, but by the Spirit's prompting we must have the courage to speak out in the name of Jesus, literally and without embarrassment. Then the way will open up in front of us.

Postscript

A Final Challenge

We are living in extraordinary days. The rains of revival are on the way. The cloud is already much bigger than a man's hand. All over the world there is a resurgence of living Christianity. The coming in of the kingdom of God in our generation is a real possibility. Whether or not this movement of God's Spirit will finally bring the return of Jesus and the universal kingdom of God will depend on the size of our vision of Jesus, the depth of our fellowship together in the Holy Spirit and the success of our evangelism. This can be the generation.

May God use this book to that end.

If you wish to receive *regular information* about *new books*, please send your name and address to:

London Bible Warehouse
PO Box 123
Basingstoke
Hants RG23 7NL

Name ______________________________

Address ______________________________

____

____

____

I am especially interested in:

- ☐ Biographies
- ☐ Fiction
- ☐ Christian living
- ☐ Issue related books
- ☐ Academic books
- ☐ Bible study aids
- ☐ Children's books
- ☐ Music
- ☐ Other subjects

P.S. If you have ideas for new Christian Books or other products, please write to us too!